To Jim
Matt 9:37
Dave Hart

W9-COL-669

KINGDOM GAINS

What Every Christian Should Know
Before Investing, and How to use Socially
and Biblically Responsible Investments
(BRI) as a Steward of God's Money

By Dwight L. Short

First Edition
First Printing Version 1.0.3

More information online at
KingdomGains.com

Published by

GShort.com, LLC
Burbank, OH

Copyright ©2010 by Dwight L. Short All rights reserved. No part of this publication may be reproduced, distributed, or transmitted in any form or by any means, including photocopying, recording, or other electronic or mechanical methods, without the prior written permission of the publisher, except in the case of brief quotations embodied in critical reviews and certain other noncommercial uses permitted by copyright law. For permission requests, write to the publisher, addressed "Attention: Permissions Coordinator," at the address below.

GShort.com, LLC
13962 Gearhart Rd
Burbank, OH 44214
www.gshort.com (330)439-2025

Ordering Information: ISBN-13: 978-0-9845366-4-1   ISBN-10: 0-9845366-4-7
1-50 books can be ordered online at KingdomGains.com or from your favorite bookstore. Extended discounts are available on quantity (50+) purchases by corporations, associations, and others. For details, contact the publisher at the address above.
Orders by U.S. trade bookstores and wholesalers can be made through Ingram Book Distribution.
Printed in the United States of America

Although the author and publisher have made every effort to ensure that the information in this book was correct at press time, the author and publisher do not assume and hereby disclaim any liability to any party for any loss, damage, or disruption caused by errors or omissions, whether such errors or omissions result from negligence, accident, or any other cause. The information that appears in this book is not a solicitation to buy or sell any security. You should consult with your own financial advisor before making any major financial decisions, including investments or changes to your portfolio. All marks, brands, and names belong to the respective companies and manufacturers and are used solely to identify the companies and products.

Unless otherwise noted, Scripture is from the HOLY BIBLE, NEW INTERNATIONAL VERSION® NIV®. Copyright 1973, 1978, 1984 by International Bible Society®. Used by permission of International Bible Society®. All rights reserved worldwide.

Investment Management Consultants Association is the owner of the certification mark "CIMA®", and the service mark "Certified Investment Managment Analyst℠. The use of these marks signifies that the user has successfully completed IMCA's initial and ongoing credentialing requirements for investment management consultants.

Book Design and Layout by GShort.com, LLC
Cover Design by Bruce Gore, Gore Studio Inc. http://gorestudio.com
Editing by Kima Jude
Proofreading by Kinney Cathcart

Publisher's Cataloging-in-Publication data
CIP Data forthcoming. See http://www.KingdomGains.com/CIF
PCN: 2010907095

This work is dedicated to my wife and family
who have endured the many years of my writing
and have still encouraged me; to the advisors
who have sacrificially worked to bring BRI to the
world; and to each member of all my mission
teams who has prayed for me and supported me
in making *Kingdom Gains* a reality.

Dwight Short
2010

FOREWORD BY RON BLUE

One of the greatest challenges that we face as Christians is how to integrate our faith into our financial decision-making. Some things are obvious to us such as tithing. What is less obvious is how to make our investment decisions faith-based. There are two aspects to this; one is the process that we use, and the second is the actual investment or investment vehicle that we use.

Over the last several years a discipline of evaluating investments and investment vehicles has been developed using what are called screens. This was first introduced by those who wanted to adopt certain social screens to their investments. They were concerned about environmental and other moral issues and did not want their investments to be used for purposes that they considered to be contrary to their value system.

For many years a Christian investor had no way of making investments reflecting their biblical worldview. This has changed dramatically in the last several years as techniques and tools have been developed to apply biblical worldview screens to the investment decision. For years many denominations and ministries have been able to make investments that were consistent with their moral values. The difficulty for the average investor has been that they did not have enough money to entice the money managers to individually screen their investments.

Today there are many mutual funds that employ moral and biblical screens to the investments they make. In addition there are many professional financial advisors such as Dwight Short who have been able to assist their clients in making investment decisions consistent with their biblical worldview. Dwight has not only been a very, very successful investment advisor, but he is a

I have made every attempt to contact and interview a wide range of people in my desire to present this issue fairly. I especially salute the heroes of this industry who have stepped out in faith to build organizations and firms which provide services that will allow investors to hire competent money managers who are screening their holdings with an eternal purpose. Although this book does not endorse any single provider cited, I confess at the outset that I have used and will continue to expand my use of many of these investment professionals to handle portions of the funds that the Lord has entrusted to me. It is important for you to know, however, that I have tried to interview each as an objective third party, and you should conduct your own research before deciding on any investment or money manager. This book is intended to be a guide as to how to do the research, and is not in any way an attempt to market or advertise for any manager.

When I rededicated my life to Christ as a teenager, I adopted Matthew 6:33 as my life philosophy: "But seek first his kingdom and his righteousness, and all these things will be given to you as well." I trust that this book will be another extension of that idea. If it offends you, pray about it. If it challenges you, pray about it. If you don't want to even think about this because it seems too much to grasp, I will pray for you!

INTRODUCTION

Dennis Kozlowski of Tyco, Joe Nacchio, CEO of Quest International, and Bernie Ebbers of WorldCom all received hundreds of millions of dollars in compensation and have since been convicted of fraudulent activities. Michael Eisner of the Walt Disney Company, Robert Nardelli of Home Depot and countless other corporate chieftains also have been paid hundreds of millions of dollars, even though through legal means. Did you know that you may have approved all of their payouts? Through stock ownership or investments in mutual funds, the shareholder approvals for outrageous compensation for these and other companies top executives have been a part of the corporate excesses for many years.

It is estimated that one million babies were aborted last year, and the profits from such procedures as well as other related industries are in the billions. Did you benefit from that by investing in companies who perform those services and offer those products?

How about pornography and child pornography? Did you invest in companies that benefited from this dramatic growth industry? Does it matter that your capital is being used for advancing this type of company, in the mutual funds you own?

If you are one of the millions of Christians who reads and acknowledges the Bible to be the central way God communicates with man about all sorts of things, including money, then this book will give you some valuable insights—and the answer to a question you may not otherwise have thought to ask: What is Biblically Responsible Investing, and why should I adopt it?

Biblically Responsible Investing, or BRI, as it is often referred to, is the act of seeking the Lord's will and honoring God in all aspects of our investment experiences.

In the U.S., from 2000 to 2020 as the wealthiest generation in the history of the world in terms of assets, the baby boomers will begin transferring their wealth to the next generation. The estimated value of this generational shift—trillions of dollars—is staggering, especially when one considers whether these vast sums of money are being used or will be used for the glory of God. Could the Great Commission be funded and realized in this generation if just 10 percent of this vast sum were to be given to Kingdom causes?

Much has already been written about legacy planning and how to avoid spoiling and corrupting heirs with this wealth; this book does not delve into that subject. Instead, the focus of this book is on what God has entrusted to you. *Kingdom Gains* is based on some simple but rock-solid truths:

- The Bible is God's Holy Word.
- The possessions you have are a blessing from God.
- Possessions carry with them the responsibility to handle them in a way that pleases God.
- Generosity and giving are models God has given us in abundant examples.
- How we pass our wealth to the next generation could determine the timing of the fulfillment of the Great Commission.
- God owns it all.
- If you can't argue with these statements, let me challenge you to connect the dots by considering these questions: What would Jesus want you to do with your possessions and blessings? If stocks are included in those holdings, what stocks, if any, would He purchase? How would He handle the proxy that arrives in the mail or over the Internet to approve stock options? What would Jesus do if He finds out the company

in which He's a shareholder helps fund abortions or pornography or engages in actions in direct conflict with His
teachings?

Confronted with these dizzying scenarios, doing a good job
managing God's money, especially in the area of investments,
suddenly may seem much more complicated. Yet the answers to
these and other questions fall into the realm of the Christian who
seeks to glorify the Lord in all he does, including his investment
activities. A Christian investor also might consider the entreaty
offered by Pope Benedict XVI when he urged companies to look
at their employees as people participating in a process rather than
commodities and mere instruments of production.

Even if you subscribe to the theory that Jesus would not bother
investing in any stock because He would give all worldly wealth
to the poor, you must acknowledge that God chooses wealth as a
means to bless some—Solomon is an Old Testament example—for
the very purpose of using it for His Kingdom. Moreover, in the
New Testament parable of the talents taught by Jesus (Matt 25:14-
30), pursuit of wealth was an expectation. Therefore, it would
be short-sighted and wasteful to ignore the potential for *Kingdom
Gains* by refusing to consider any investment activity. The perti-
nent question for us as believers then becomes: How can I invest
my money responsibly in accordance with biblical standards?

An oft-used, shorter version of the definition of BRI comes
from an affinity group of Kingdom Advisors and is based on 1
Corinthians 10:31:"Investing that seeks to glorify God as an act
of worship."

I invite you to thoroughly explore BRI with me through the
pages of this book and determine if changes are merited in your
investment habits. I fully expect that after reading this book, you
will analyze every potential new investment as well as review all
the holdings you currently have, against, not just the bottom line,

years, but I simply had not considered filtering investments as this group did. In addition, the Timothy Plan highlighted sinful activities conducted by companies on issues I had never contemplated.

It was interesting stuff, but as my company had no selling agreement with this organization, I couldn't really show it to my clients. I set it aside.

The people at Timothy Plan kept my contact information, however, and soon invited me to a conference with other Christian advisors. By this time my wife and I had purchased our second home in Florida, and I really loved hiding out there a few weeks every year. My initial response was to decline, claiming I would be too busy. When I discovered, however, that the conference was being conducted within a 20-minute drive from where I lived in Florida, I signed up.

My life as a financial consultant has never been the same! I quickly discovered that people attending this conference were much more serious about integrating their faith into their practice than I had been. They hammered home the idea that God owns everything, and, although I had thought that sounded good in principle, I realized I had never fully embraced this concept. After all, surely that couldn't have been God prompting me to pick up the phone to make cold calls and prospect for clients for my first 10 years in the business? I wanted to take credit for the growth in my clients' assets and success of being a million-dollar producer. While I tried to be humble about all the blessings that came my way, the country and western song rang true for me: "Oh Lord, it's hard to be humble, when you're perfect in every way!" Obviously, I needed a lot of help!

At the conference we received books about how Christians are called to deal with money and wealth. Reading Randy Alcorn's *The Treasure Principle and Money Possessions and Eternity* was an epiphany for me. Prior to this, my success had been measured by worldly standards.

Little did I know then, that God soon would reinforce the lesson that this world's standards are temporary and fragile. Any hubris built up in my persona from the bull market in stocks from 1981 to 2000 evaporated in the years from 2001 to 2002, when stocks fell sharply. I was even further humbled by market setbacks during the 2008 debacle when the credit crunch hit real estate, stocks and almost every financial asset other than bonds. The biblical teachings outlined in this conference rang true. God does own it all! And He can give it and take it away in a heartbeat. I was learning to look beyond the temporal earthly value of every asset to discover its eternal dividends.

I realized anew that my successes as a financial consultant had not been due to my ability but God's timing and blessing. More important, the conviction grew that it was vital that I manage money in a way that adhered to biblical values as worship to God—and lead others to do it as well. From that conference the National Association of Christian Financial Consultants, better known as the NACFC, was born. I enlisted and became a card-carrying member.

GOD CARES HOW YOU INVEST YOUR MONEY!

If you live in America and are invested in a mutual fund—even if you never buy stocks as an individual—you, too, are a stakeholder in the investment arena. You must learn to think of yourself this way.

But if you're reading this book because you are a Christian investor, your responsibility is much bigger; indeed, yours is a sacred duty. Even if your participation up until now has been limited to biannual glimpses of your portfolio, you're not off the hook. Investing biblically is your responsibility. As an investor/owner of publicly traded companies, it's up to you to know whether the company in which you are a shareholder measures up to God's standards. Let's think about what this entails:

If a company promotes the homosexual lifestyle, sells pornography, profits from gambling, produces alcohol, tobacco or abortion tools or uses abusive tactics in its employment practices, do you think God cares if you own stock in it?

I decided to take a poll among professional investment managers whose job it is to make investments utilizing screens to filter out undesirable companies that operate outside of biblical values. The companies to which we applied these screens are the same ones listed daily in the New York Times, compiled by the Associated Press and called "The Favorites." This means they are among the most widely held stocks of clients who have their securities at Merrill Lynch/Bank of America.

This exercise was not intended to indicate in any way whether these stocks should be bought, sold or exchanged and any discussion in this book about specific stocks is not any type of buy-or-sell recommendation. You should always consult a financial advisor before making changes to your holdings. With that noted, let's take a look at The Favorites:

- Alcatel Lucent
- Bank of America
- Apple
- AT & T, Inc
- Chevron
- Citigroup
- Cisco
- Comcast
- Disney
- ExxonMobil
- General Electric
- IBM
- Intel
- Johnson and Johnson
- JP Morgan Chase
- Microsoft
- Pfizer
- Procter & Gamble
- Time Warner
- Verizon Communications
- Home Depot (replaced by Idearc in 2007)

Table 1-A BRI Company investments in "The Favorites"					
Company	Stewardship Partners		Timothy Plan		Ave Maria	
Investment Status	OWN	Violations	OWN	Violations	OWN	Violations
Apple Computer	NO	4	NO	NA	NO	YES
AT&T Corporation	NO	8	NO	9	NO	YES
Bank of America	NO	3	NO	8	NO	YES
Chevron	NO	3	NO	8	NO	NO
Cisco	YES	0	NO	9	NO	YES
Citigroup	NO	3	NO	8	NO	YES
Comcast	NO	4	NO	5	NO	YES
Walt Disney Corp	NO	3	NO	11	NO	YES
ExxonMobil	NO	0	YES	0	YES	NO
General Electric	NO	4	NO	10	NO	YES
Home Depot	NO	2	NO	5	NO	YES
Idearc	NO	NA	NO	NA	NO	NA
Intel	NO	2	NO	7	NO	YES
IBM	NO	2	NO	7	NO	YES
JP MorganChase	NO	3	NO	9	NO	YES
Johnson & Johnson	NO	4	NO	11	NO	YES
Lucent	NO	2	NO	7	NO	YES
Microsoft	NO	4	NO	9	NO	YES
Pfizer	NO	4	NO	11	NO	YES
Procter & Gamble	NO	4	NO	9	NO	YES
Time Warner	NO	4	NO	11	NO	YES
Verizon	NO	3	NO	8	NO	YES

do not typically consider investing in these "favorite holdings." They also indicated that when they do add a large cap component to their portfolio, the companies and the violations listed above would still apply.

CHECK YOUR PORTFOLIO

As you check to see if you are already a shareholder in some of these companies, you may be in for a nasty surprise: **You may have investments in a company that violates biblical principles!** Take comfort: This great awakening may be just what you need to move you to see God work in another part of your life—your investments!

How should you react to this unwelcome revelation? Should you make the radical move of immediately selling all such assets and withdraw completely from investing? (How does one do that in today's world anyway?) Or should you simply ignore your new-found knowledge and look the other way?

It is common for some well-meaning Christians to take a defensive position over their investments because the offending companies also may be lauded as leaders of American industry. They participate in our dynamic economy with growth and productivity, and they have provided paychecks and comfortable retirement plans for many people.

That doesn't excuse them, however, if they are sponsoring activities that oppose Christianity. The sad fact is, the likelihood that you own one or more of these stocks is quite high unless you already have done your homework and researched these companies to discover what they are doing in all areas of their corporate outreach. Even if you don't own these stocks individually, if you invest in mutual funds it is still very likely that your fund will own many of these companies.

As a shareholder, you are a fractional owner in that company. As a Christian shareholder, you have an additional responsibility to act as God's proxy. Consider this: By always giving approval for any proposal of management, you have helped endorse the actions of that company. Voting with management without thinking about the consequences has been a longstanding tradition that the managements of public corporations take into consideration and rely upon. By throwing your proxy in the wastebasket or automatically marking it with management, you may have been unwittingly complicit to sinful activities conducted by corporate America today.

In the chapters ahead I will show you how to take the steps necessary to conform to Biblically Responsible Investing and become better stewards of all that God has given to you. Meanwhile, let's take a hard look at how companies may be failing God—and we as shareholders may be failing them.

THE BIBLICAL CASE AGAINST CORPORATE AMERICA

Among this list there are several companies who annually make large donations to Planned Parenthood, offer same-sex benefits or subsidize entertainment that is beyond X-rated. Almost all offer executive compensation plans that are out of control.

Just as it should be noted that we have chosen these companies at random and that many screeners find violations, I also want to point out that in all likelihood there are Christians employed at all of these companies who labor there daily in an effort to be salt and light. Despite their efforts, however, companies have incurred the following descriptions that should lead Christian investors and BRI providers to want to know more about the policies of the corporations in which they are purchasing stock. These are the descriptions you will find from the BRI screenings that define some of these activities. Understand that this is not to be a broadbrush approach to all companies and all violations but a sampling

A significant client account back then might contain $100,000 in assets, and as I impatiently explained this complicated investment to the caller, I asked how much he was thinking of purchasing. His reply: "Three million dollars worth!"

A few days later, my new favorite client deposited $5 million and purchased $3 million in short-term notes. The other $2 million became the base for various investments that he entrusted to me for the next 32 years of my employment. I always thought that God had blessed me in ways beyond my comprehension, but this was like winning the lottery! As a Christian, I have always thanked God for this blessing, but now I understand more fully that it happened for a reason.

When I retired from Merrill Lynch more than 30 years later, Marvin was still a trusted and wonderful client who sent me at least 10 other clients as referrals. Now, looking back, I must acknowledge that gaining this account early in my career was simply confirmation of the calling on my life then and now: teaching financial investments that honor God. God had blessed me at a time when the survival rate of my colleagues was very low for a purpose. Many brokers left the business because of low productivity. The financial markets then were producing mostly negative returns for anyone holding stocks, and interest rates were in double digits.

With newfound awareness of BRI, I have grown more confident that God has more work for me to do in financial services.

You may be experiencing the curse of wealth that keeps you from seeing God's will for your life and your money. If you have placed your confidence in your net worth, your job or your position, then God will be shaking your confidence soon! Who gave you life and the intellect to make deals, build companies and invest in public and private ventures?

A dear friend, Maxton Sutton of Covenant Concepts, is my best example of someone who believes deeply that God owns it all. A few years ago he and his wife Jeannette decided to take this idea seriously. Accordingly, they added Jesus Christ, our Lord and Savior, to the name and address portion of their checks.

I have often wondered about the discussion that took place at the printers when they got this request from Maxton and printed that first set of checks. Imagine with me, however, how this has changed the dynamics of all of their transactions! Maxton will relate to you how this works when things don't go right and mix-ups and mistakes take place in the middle of trying to complete a transaction that's being fumbled badly. How difficult it is when you want to let some error-prone clerk have the wrath of your righteous indignation when you have the Lord's name at the top of your check and you plan on paying for the purchase with one of those checks!

WHY IS THIS SO DIFFICULT FOR US?

It's hard to accept the concept that God owns it all because we want to think of ourselves as being in control of our lives and our assets. This tendency for self-reliance and rebellion against anything that makes us accountable is counter to our human instincts for independence. The sooner we can recognize God's sovereignty, the easier it will be to exercise our role in acting with a "limited power of attorney" (limited by our lifetime) to represent God's interests as we seek His will. This would include all areas of financial management and, once we become shareholders, demands that we seek to be Biblically Responsible Investors.

Just as Maxton was reminded every time he and his wife wrote a check that they must ask themselves how God would want them to spend this money, we as investors must first ask how God would invest His money. When it comes time to vote our proxies, we have to decide how God would want us to act in properly holding the management teams of our companies accountable when it comes to corporate governance issues.

If you are still in doubt about who owns all of our "stuff," check out some of these passages:

> *In the same way, any of you who does not give up everything he has cannot be my disciple. Salt is good, but if it loses its saltiness, how can it be made salty again? (Luke 14:33-34)*

The context of this is not a demand for divestment of all of our assets but recognition of who owns them. If you cannot admit that God owns them, you are not capable of being salt and light to others in your dealings.

Howard Dayton in his book *Your Money Counts* points to 1 Chronicles 29:11-12:

> *Yours, O Lord, is the greatness and the power and the glory and the majesty and splendor, for everything in heaven and earth is yours. Yours, O Lord, is the kingdom; you are exalted as head over all. Wealth and honor come from you; you are the ruler of all things. In your hands are strength and power to exalt and give strength to all.*

WE HAVE BEEN TOO PASSIVE AS SHAREHOLDERS

By this point, it already should be obvious that most of us have fallen short in our duties and responsibilities as they relate to being responsible Christian shareholders. By conceding the moral ground to others who neither read nor care about biblical truth, we have allowed a secular society to force moral principles upon us that brought sexual sin; materialism and impurity of all types to a level of acceptance that now require us to recover this "stolen" property. By not acknowledging the environmental and ecological waste that we are causing, surely we have displeased God with how we are maintaining his perfect creation. Because of the selfish and outrageous compensation levels that are being handed out of the corporate boardrooms while the average worker faces health care and retirement benefit deficiencies, God must wonder where the saltiness has gone.

Are you ready to make a difference and become part of a movement of Christians in America who are not going to accept business as usual? Or are you a professional in the financial services industry who has been trained to be oblivious to the moral and spiritual issues of corporate life? Have you been an undercover Christian afraid to stand your moral ground on these issues?

You will meet many people on the pages of this book who will inspire you to stop being so negligent in your faith and understand that doing what Jesus would do at the office and with your investments can and will make a difference. God bless you as you read on and pray about how the Lord needs to work in your life. Please consider the words of Ken Boa and this excerpt from the book, *Holistic Spirituality, Stewardship and Purpose*:

> We have seen that holistic spirituality involves a growing responsiveness to the Lordship of Christ in every internal and external facet of our lives. It is not a question of developing a list of theoretical priorities (e.g., God first, family second, work and ministry third, etc.), but more a matter of allowing the centrality of Christ to determine and empower what we should do in each day. Seen this way, Christ is our Life and Lord in all our activities, and whatever we are doing at the moment becomes our priority focus. When the grace of Christ rules in our lives, we will better discern how to allocate the resources God has entrusted to us.

It seems obvious that we cannot separate our investing activities from the rest of our walk with the Lord.

QUESTIONS TO CONSIDER

1. Do you really think God cares how we make money? If so, how does that apply to your own situation? Did you notice any of the companies listed in the Favorites List as one in which you have invested? Have you ever had occasion to do business with any of them?

2. How do you feel about the idea that God owns it all? Would you be able to change the name on your checks to include Jesus?

3. When you consider the ideas presented by Ken Boa on the way God permeates everything we do, are there aspects of your life that you find hard to relate to that?If so, what and why?

2

SHOULD THE CHURCH CARE?

The topic of finances is the one pastors most avoid. Fear of ser-
mons on money is the chief excuse for not attending church and
not bringing guests. And today's seminaries, by their own admis-
sion, are extremely reluctant to take the lead in helping pastors
and church leaders learn how to become better stewards.
Wes Willmer, Ph.D. Biola University

Growing up on a farm in Northwestern Ohio, my days of work
and chores were regularly interrupted by Sunday morning and
evening church services at the Evangelical Mennonite Church in
Wauseon. Oh, yes, there also were Thursday mid-week services
requiring my presence each week. But it was a revival that stands
out in my memory because it was scheduled daily for a whole
week!

tions of the investment and corporate world's long reach into the lives of their church members.

THE RELEVANT CHURCH KNOWS FINANCES

As simplistic as this may read, the moral issues surrounding financial investments and other critical issues facing the average man or woman in the pew often go unaddressed in today's churches. I have heard this era in the Christian church often characterized as light on substance and heavy on appearances. I can't help but notice that the mega church seems to be the fastest-growing segment on the evangelical landscape, while mainline churches appear to be falling on hard times as their memberships dwindle. The reason that many of these "seeker" churches have gone the route of rock bands and high tech attractions is that their people demand a different and more modern experience. While mainline churches are left to defend the relevancy of their message, seeker churches similarly are often called to defend themselves about their depth of teaching. Yet, to my way of thinking, both mainline and mega churches are missing the mark when dealing with some important moral considerations, especially in the realm of BRI.

The deeper issues that relate to this problem are the concepts of biblical stewardship and materialism. I am convinced that churches and pastors who believe the Bible to be the inspired Word of God would find great practical applications for their members if they could approach both concepts with more knowledge and firepower. Frankly, however, preaching on money, stewardship or investing seems to make most pastors want to run away and hide.

HARD MONEY FACTS FOR THE SUNDAY SERMON

I've realized that sermons or messages that deal with money issues in a thorough way are difficult because it is rarely an area of expertise for most pastors, often because they grew up in families of modest means where investing never has been a priority topic. Add to that the lack of training from seminaries on financial planning and investments and pastors don't know how to talk about—let alone preach with conviction on—investing. In addition, churches and their elders have been known to underpay their pastors to an extent that their ability to have enough savings to invest also is a rarity; therefore, many clergy cannot address the subject from personal experience.

Perhaps the most compelling reason that pastors don't rush into the subject of money and investing is that many of their congregants complain that the "church is always asking for money." Indeed, that may be a sad commentary on the very real need for pastors to learn about this subject.

Also contributing to the problem is the false teaching that has emanated from the pulpit on such issues as Y2K as well as misinformation about end times. Some of the financial crises prophesied have bordered on scare tactics, and one has to wonder if they weren't conjured up to sell something.

Because of this, it would be easy for an earnest, well-intentioned pastor to decide not to add to these unfortunate impressions by refusing to interfere in the financial area that involves people's stocks and mutual funds. I would even go so far as to say that avoiding this topic is so common, many churchgoers can safely expect to hear the traditional sermon on money only once or twice a year—or when a giving campaign rolls around.

Certainly pastors have priorities, and I admire them for their efforts in evangelism, shepherding, preaching and missions. In fact, to not be overly concerned about money is to a pastor's credit. No one wants a pastor who is focused on the secular, physical or carnal.

But a pastor who has committed himself to shepherding his flock and providing his church with guidance in the real world cannot ignore the subject either. My pastor, Rick Duncan of

Cuyahoga Valley Church in Cleveland, Ohio, explains it well. He points out that Acts 6 tells us that deacons ought to handle the practical affairs of the church to free up pastors to focus on the Word. If pastors identify the prayer needs of the believers and bring biblical truth from the pulpit on those subjects, they will have served their flock well. Yet how should we expect these same servants of God to gain insights in the world of investing when they are to be focused on prayer and the Word?

My solution would be to have more financial advisors act in the manner of a deacon by sharing their expertise in their home churches, and the understanding level of pastors would rise accordingly. Once a pastor has been helped in this way, it will give more credibility to his preaching and teaching on money and investments. Encouraging these same financial professionals to join together with other Christians in Kingdom Advisors and the National Association of Christian Financial Consultants also will bring greater awareness and effectiveness in their professional workplaces.

Ric Cannada, chancellor of Reformed Theological Seminary, believes that the church today is characterized by Christians who are greatly unfamiliar with biblical truth. He blames the lack of interest in Biblically Responsible Investing on a larger problem: Many Christians are so young in the faith and so little schooled in the truth of the Bible that we are unable to relate or apply these principles in our lives. If we simply knew the Word, the case for BRI would be more easily made.

I am pleased to learn that many mega churches have realized this and have attempted with varying success to start small groups or community groups to fill this void and bring biblical substance to the new modern worship experience. Yet it doesn't take a mega congregation filled with financial experts to teach and train others in this area. It takes merely one person.

SERMON STARTERS ON FINANCIAL INVESTING

Fortunately, a large amount of study material has already been developed in this area, and many useful resources can be obtained to help in the teaching of the subject of stewardship. For example, Pastor Pat Hail, formerly of West Greenway Baptist Church in Glendale, Arizona and now the pastor/director of development for the Christian Financial Association of America, has found that the materials offered through Biblical Stewardship Seminars and Inductive Bible Study have made a huge impact on believers. Many of these studies and resources are offered by Precept Ministries International and can be obtained easily through Internet contact.

The key point is that spiritual people of influence in the church must provide leadership by practicing BRI in their own lives and inspiring others to do so as well. Other ministries that are making great contributions to the effort include Crown Ministries, Generous Giving, Financial Peace University, Stewardship International and the Willow Creek Association, among others. Although pastors usually take the lead in any kind of teaching, let me be quick to point out that this is one area where both pastors and believers may be learning about these issues together (See Appendix A for information on these ministries).

THE PASTOR'S RETIREMENT FUND TELLS ITS OWN STORY

If you as a pastor or other spiritual leader are still not motivated by the concept of BRI, let me put it in terms that should convince you that it's a subject you cannot afford to ignore. Think about how your own retirement funds are invested. One pastor told me he thought this was a no-brainer because he invested all his funds through an association of his denomination. Surely they would be

In Isaiah 28:23-29 we are reminded of the importance of understanding each process a farmer goes through: He cultivates the soil, plants the seeds, then exercises patience to let the seed grow until the thrashing or harvest time finally arrives. Once the wheat is harvested and made into bread, it is not necessary to keep thrashing and pounding the same seed any longer.

I believe that the concept of BRI is in the seed-planting stage as most people remain unaware of the need or responsibility that Christians have in representing their Lord and Savior in the selection of stocks and mutual funds that reflect their Christian worldview or when voting their proxy. You, as the spiritual leaders of the church, can help by placing this issue alongside all of the other responsibilities we have as good stewards of God's gifts.

One of the best resources you can tap into for this issue is other pastors with personal experience in BRI. Many can share how they have approached the preaching aspects of stewardship and BRI as well as divestment strategies from retirement plans that do not embrace BRI. Pastors also are eager to share with others when they have found good resources that have worked for their congregation. Therefore, you will find a list of pastors and resources listed in Appendix A, along with contact information. You probably don't need me to remind you of this, but I will anyway: Romans 14 teaches that each man must be convinced for himself of God's calling, and this is why we all have the lights click on about truth at different times in our lives. My prayer is that this particular light is clicking on for you right now.

THE FINANCIAL ADVISOR IN YOUR CHURCH

Another great resource that exists today may be sitting right in front of you in that thousands of Christian financial advisors have studied and been certified to help teach in the local church and to properly advise Christian clients about how to bring a biblical perspective to one's investing activities. It would benefit you greatly to encourage all the members of your church who are employed in the financial services to join together with other financial professionals and become part of the organized believers who are trying to bring this issue to the investing public. The two primary organizations who are working to enlist members from this industry are the NACFC and Kingdom Advisors, formerly known as CFPN (Christian Financial Professionals Network). Appendix A provides contact information to search out people who are working in close proximity to your part of the country who could help you and your church. The men and women of these organizations have been trained to be servants to churches and not merely to use their positions to gain access to people and their funds in order to promote their own selfish agendas. No doubt this has and always will be a concern anytime you ask someone to help in this regard.

The history of NACFC goes back to the late 1990s when Art Ally, who was the founder of the Timothy Plan mutual fund family, and six other financial advisors started the organization to challenge advisors to make their financial planning practice their ministry and not just their vocation. It currently has close to 300 members and is national in scope and relates more to advisors than other financial professionals. Kingdom Advisors, with more than 4,200 members, was started a few years later from an organization that Larry Burkett founded and, more recently, has been headed by Ron Blue. Kingdom Advisors attempts to take a broader outreach to financial professionals, including attorneys and CPAs, as well as to advisors and consultants. Both organizations have placed Christ as the head of all they do, and they work to foster greater understanding and emphasis for investors and pastors to find help in all aspects of financial planning and investing. The growth of both of these organizations is coming at a perfect time to help all investors, but especially Christians, find their way through this often complicated and difficult process of investing.

Another organization that has focused significant resources in communicating with pastors on money and how it can help is Generous Giving. Its annual conferences on money topics are geared for pastors and have been uniquely informative in areas that are missing in other events.

While you, as pastors, are among the most generous people on the face of the earth, your role in communicating investment patterns that will please the Lord cannot be overstated. Pastors are already dealing with materialism in the patterns of their congregants, and the investment patterns are an extension of that condition. The connection between giving to the poor and investing is intertwined within Jesus' teachings.

BEWARE THE WOLF IN SHEEP'S CLOTHING

Connecting your church and its people with Christian Financial Advisors is a wonderful idea, but I need to add a word of caution at this point: Remember that the people who work in this industry may be motivated by money. Furthermore, BRI does not promise an investor financial gains; it works toward *Kingdom Gains*. Anyone who invests in the stock market takes a financial risk. The risks can be managed to some extent, but there will always come a time when those being helped will have financial losses because the markets do not go up all the time. Good planning and sound advice cannot avoid the risk of market fluctuations, but the 800-pound gorilla in the room is the isolated but rare occurrence of the fraudulent thief who may prey on praying people. Like all other realms, remember that our trust should be placed in God first and people second.

This risk is not as great as ignoring the whole area of financial accountability. But monitoring the events and activities of any advisor that is brought into your congregation is a must.

QUESTIONS TO CONSIDER

1. Do you get frustrated when your pastor talks about money?

2. Does your church interpret stewardship as being something more than just money management in regard to charitable giving? If the answer is no, do you see that as a need? If yes, what are the positives and negatives of that expanded definition?

3. Do you think pastors understand the pressures of working in the work-a-day secular world? How would you try to help someone who is in the church to understand the market-place pressures?

4. Should pastors be concerned about how their congregants invest their money?

als working among so many different companies, it's also a question investors should try to answer when seeking investment help.

There have been movements of people to join together as Christians in various walks of life to help encourage each other in the faith journey but also to help promote the cause of Christ in their vocations. In the world of the financial professionals, the NACFC and Kingdom Advisors have been leading the charge since the late '90s to enlist believers in the cause of Christ while giving financial advice or offering financial services. Prior to 2007, Kingdom Advisors had been known as the Christian Financial Professionals Network (CFPN) but recently changed its name to Kingdom Advisors as a way of distinguishing itself from organizations with other similar acronyms.

There are many committed Christians who labor in the financial services industry offering advice and managing resources for their clients, all in an effort to serve in the place God has called them. Investors can find good people in many settings and should not feel this is a book indicating that only those who don the label of "Christian Financial Advisors" are competent enough to do the job. My personal observation, however, was that Christians often preferred to work with other believers when it comes to handling the monetary blessings God has entrusted to them. On the other hand, you also may decide to choose an advisor who has no close ties. I was privileged to have a Jewish rabbi as a client. He decided it was easier to work with me rather than choosing just one of the many congregants who were advisors.

THEY'RE NOT YOUR GRANDMOTHER'S FINANCIAL SERVICES

My starting point in working as a financial advisor began in 1971 when God called me from the work I had been doing as a teacher and coach and planted me in the midst of one of the world's largest brokerage firms. I would need to write a separate book to describe fully what life was like back then in the world of investing. Suffice it to say, it bore little resemblance to what is happening today. A very busy day back then would be to have *total* volume for all stocks on the New York Stock Exchange (NYSE) at 5,000,000 shares. Today that is often less than the volume for one stock among the 50 most active issues, and total volume is measured in hundreds of millions of shares.

Brokerage firms were considered quite speculative then because almost all of their revenue came from commissions and fees related to the trading of individual stocks and bonds. In fact, the more trading that was done, the more profitable the brokerage firms would be and also the more money the "customers' men" would take home as their income. This conflict of interest existed early on in the brokerage industry and was a constant and compelling theme in evaluating the honesty and integrity of the people. It still exists today but to a much lesser extent with the advent of giving clients the choice of fees or commissions as a way of paying for financial services. The range of product choices today also allows advisors to sell insured Certificates of Deposit right alongside the higher risk investments. In light of the billions of losses the Wall Street firms have taken in 2008, it would appear that not all of their diversification moves have been prudent. The individual investment advisors, however, are still most easily found at these large firms.

THE CHANGING FACE OF RETIREMENT SAVINGS

Another major difference between life in the '70s and life today for financial advisors is that people are seeking more help than ever before in dealing with the complications of the investment choices facing them. The majority of people in 1970 worked for companies or in service areas that would provide a "guaranteed" pension with a fixed benefit. The same pension income also would be accompanied by a cost-of-living increase to help offset inflation. This was often in addition to the "guaranteed" benefit

49

of Social Security payments that still seemed quite safe in comparison to today's expectations. Industrial jobs in the auto, steel and machinery companies were plentiful, and although wage inflation due to the strength of union solidarity caused concern about the declining value of the dollar, life seemed fairly simple for the average citizen.

Many of those same guaranteed benefits have more recently been changed, lost or eliminated by companies as well as by government agencies, thus making it more important than ever to plan ahead for one's own retirement. There was not as much demand for financial planning at that time because the predictability of retirement income was being calculated at the union hall, by the corporate benefit departments or by the government at the local Social Security office. Most people were not relying on an investment strategy or a financial planner to make their retirement budget work. If there was a post-war trend that appealed to the masses, it was the idea of having your own home. Inflation was very high, but homes seemed to hold their value. This was, of course, prior to the housing debacle of 2002 to 2008. As a percentage of household wealth, securities, such as stocks, bonds and mutual funds, were less than 5 percent of the average person's net worth.

This has all changed since then, and many people are still living in light of the great bull market in stocks that took place from 1981 until 2000. Now securities often average close to 30 percent of someone's wealth. Furthermore, the idea of security has been transcended by corporations who no longer want to offer pension plans, known as *defined benefit plans,* because the liabilities and cost to maintain them have been usurped by other priorities. Another reason for the higher percentage is that the retirement nest eggs of people are tied up in 401(k) s, 403(b) s or what is known as defined contribution funds. The government has maintained its defined benefit plan known as Social Security, despite the fact that they may not be able to afford it, either. Even as the politicians continue to argue about who will pay for the guarantees, the funds get smaller and smaller to back up the payments, and the people funding the payments get fewer and fewer. The combination of political gridlock and lack of courage to own up to the real issues has cost valuable time in what could have been done to change the plan from a pass-through system to a fully funded system with defined benefits.

But this book is not an attempt to propose a solution for Social Security; it communicates my desire to point out the drastic differences that people are facing today in the uncertainty of their retirement benefits, along with the need for people to plan ahead in such an uncertain environment.

SAY GOOD-BYE TO THE DREAM OF NEVER WORKING AGAIN

Another mega trend that exists in the American culture today is the contrast in economic styles of different generations. In his book *The Greatest Generation*, Tom Brokaw points out the incredible willingness for people of that era to pay the ultimate sacrifice of life and limb to defend our country and fight for the freedoms that our forefathers envisioned. The descendants of that Greatest Generation are quite different, in that they have enjoyed the freedoms to an even greater extent than the people who fought for them and established the pattern of greatness in and after World War II. Their spoiled trust-fund children and grandchildren also are the beneficiaries of a post-war boom and the stock market explosion that saw wealth grow by a multiple of 10 times. In round numbers, the Dow Jones Industrial Average of 30 largest industrial companies was 1,000 in 1981 and over 11,000 in 2001 (now fluctuating between 11,000 and 13,000 some seven years after hitting 11,000 in 2001). Even after the steep and scary stock markets plunges of 2007 through 2009, the market is still clustered around 10,000 as measured by the DJIA.

investment decision for your clients based on your biblical calling to service, let this be your epiphany and starting point. Draw your line in the sand right now and vow that this is the time and place where you will not compromise any longer. Resolve that the most biblical kinds of companies and investments are the only ones you will recommend. In fact, let me lead you in a prayer right now. Don't be afraid to read these words aloud:

Heavenly Father, forgive me for not including your Word in all of my actions and recommendations as a financial advisor. I ask that you would both guide me and bring along believers to encourage me as I seek your will for all of my clients. Give me the courage, respect and boldness to share your Word by both my speech and my actions so that clients, colleagues and those around me would see You through me. Amen.

If you've heard that every sermon has three points and a prayer, here are three challenges that I feel compelled to extend to Christian financial advisors:

- Join with other Christian financial professionals.
- Find ways to purge your clients' holdings of companies that are not consistent with Christian values.
- Learn all you can about estate planning techniques and help your clients leave a Christian legacy.

Furthermore, find out if there is a local branch of Kingdom Advisors or a member of the NACFC close by and call that person and have lunch together with him or her. These local branches will meet either monthly or quarterly, and you will find great support from them as well as from the materials you may receive from the national headquarters of their organizations. As a member of both organizations, it is easy for me to recommend either or both and trust that your time spent will be as valuable as my involvement has been with both organizations. Both of them have national conventions each year that are inspiring and very helpful to one's Christian walk while also developing vocational expertise. Each organization has training and certification procedures that are extremely valuable in giving long-term guidance to your practice and your purpose. In addition, each organization is loaded with committed Christians who want to see the Lord glorified in every way.

If you are charged with helping a client purchase and structure specific investments to help shape the portfolio holdings, this is one of the most important times for you to know what is going on in the corporate world today. Many companies have hidden the ugly side of their greed from view while forging ahead with business practices that simply could not possibly be approved by Christ. It is time for you to start learning what you can do to help your clients screen out companies that are conducting themselves in this way.

WHAT THE INVESTOR NEEDS FROM A CHRISTIAN ADVISOR

What do Christian financial advisors bring to the marketplace? If you are an investor, here is a list of questions to ask to help you identify a financial advisor who is interested in bringing Christianity into his practice:

- Does your advisor ever ask you about your faith journey to see if it is important in how you are investing your funds?
- Is there a clear channel of communication in regard to how your advisor charges for their services? (Commissions, fees, expenses for services, etc.)
- Has your advisor indicated any experience in screening investment choices to reflect a Christian worldview?
- Would your advisor pray with you and ask God's blessings on you?
- Do you feel confident that your advisor is looking at you instead of your money?
- Would you trust this advisor to help your children, grandchildren or a sick relative?

- Is this advisor knowledgeable in a wide variety of subjects, especially in finance?

This is actually a good list for an advisor of any stripe, but it is even more important that your Christian advisor be able to pass most of these questions easily.

It has been a long time since the days of my being hired into the brokerage industry along with the people who were, alas, often referred to as "money-grubbing scum." People get hired today for reasons that are much different from 1970. The bottom line though remains the bottom line. Advisors must be productive, and investors must always be vigilant to ensure that what is being done is for their own good.

Advisors are asked by their firm to prepare a sales plan each year. Advisors who are part of a team spend time on planning at the start of a new year and periodically review their progress on how well they are performing according to the sales objectives. There are many resources available for helping advisors be more deliberate in that planning. Meanwhile, check out Appendix B for additional ideas and contact information.

Many Christian advisors have added a wrinkle to that sales plan that includes helping out with the financial concerns of their church as well as ministries in their circle of influence. Some have started to work more closely with local Christian community foundations to help their clients consider leaving a financial legacy as part of their witness. I heartily applaud that initiative! My suggestion would be, in addition to adopting a Bible verse as your theme for life, try to find the theme that God is teaching you as a financial advisor and adopt a biblical theme each year for your practice. Put it in writing. Taking that simple first step will help you become the Christian financial advisor God wants you to be.

WHAT'S A CHRISTIAN FINANCIAL CONSULTANT TO DO?

QUESTIONS TO CONSIDER

1. What is your level of trust for people who work as financial advisors? Would it increase if they are Christian financial advisors?

2. If you are working in the financial services industry, do you believe that the work you are doing is something you have been "called" to do?

3. Would you be more likely to trust an advisor who had taken special training to become qualified as a biblically-based Christian advisor? What would determine your likelihood to have trust in anyone working with you on your finances and investments?

4

How do I Get Started in BRI?

*We've put our concerns about morals and character "in a box"
and prefer to worship at the altar of the economy. If the economy
is all that matters, then we really are stupid.* Cal Thomas

When investors send in a response to a mailing or an email
inquiry from a financial services firm, their information is usually
turned over to an advisor for follow-up. In 1973 I made a follow-
up phone call to a gentleman who had requested information
about tax- free bonds. Jack was a crusty old guy who lived in a
small town in central Ohio and wanted to start an account with
me. When I called the bank he gave as a credit reference, it provided the most incredible response you can imagine. I asked the
president of the bank if he knew Jack and if he would be good for
a $5,000 purchase he was planning to make with me. The banker
started laughing and said that I would be safe opening an account

with Jack, and, as a matter of fact, Jack was responsible for almost half of the bank's deposits. He further informed me that Jack kept more than $100,000 in a checking account at all times. Jack turned out to be worth many millions of dollars.

Jack was the client every financial professional dreams of advising—but with one flaw, to my way of thinking: He never used the word money and faith in the same sentence. We had a great relationship, however, and when I retired, his son remained a wonderful client. But Jack embodied what a lot of people think about connecting moral interests with investment activity. Most people do not want to know anything more than whether their investments made money!

Here's my confession: For many years, I didn't connect those dots nearly as much as I should have, either. If I could turn back the hands of time, I would love to speak with all the people like Jack who feel this way, and give them the opportunity to confront these issues. If you are still a doubter, this chapter is intended to give you practical ways to develop a game plan on how you get started changing how you make investments. **All change starts with the heart and mind, but true change only happens when you stop doing business as usual and make the adjustments necessary so that your holdings conform to your witness.**

When considering the demands of BRI, it is important to look at the history of investing with a values or moral compass. This begins with acknowledging that BRI is a recent outgrowth from an older movement known as Socially Responsible Investing (SRI) that encompasses a much larger segment of the investment world. Although the SRI movement was founded in part by many faith-based investors, the majority of SRI players are not actually quoting or using the Bible as a direct source for developing their investment screens. If you are looking for more information on the investment types that are screening from a moral, ethical, social, spiritual or biblical point of view, there is a vast array of resources for you to research. I have chosen not to focus on all of the differences of these disciplines, but, in point of fact, many of the companies are screened out of portfolios for the same reasons. Therefore, let me also note that investors may find the readings in all of these disciplines helpful when developing a strategy and game plan.

Romans 13-14

It is important that you stop reading here and read or re-read Romans 13 and 14. What I am about to communicate needs to be set in that context. After finishing those two chapters, continue on.

There is a tendency in our society today to be contentious and look at our differences rather than our points of agreement. Be aware that as much as 50 percent of the screening that is done for SRI and BRI are the same companies. Why then the differences?

Comparing SRI and BRI investing tendencies is wrought with exceptions and overlaps in how both disciplines see their worldview, but here is a sample of how the comparisons and contrasts grid looks:

1. BRI AVOIDS COMPANIES THAT CONTRIBUTE TO PLANNED PARENTHOOD, WHILE SRI MAY INVEST IN THEM; BRI AVOIDS COMPANIES THAT PROFIT FROM OR PROMOTE ABORTIONS, WHILE SRI OFTEN HAS NO SUCH RESTRICTION.

Ellen Taylor from the Investment Management Institute who helps stage conferences for faith-based investors rightly points out that there are some groups who practice SRI but have similar screens as BRI providers on issues relating to Planned Parenthood and abortion. These may include Catholic and Mormon groups as well as other faith-based ministries. Those groups have been practicing a form of SRI for many years and do not at this time use terms such as "biblical" in their explanation of screening. Other non-faith based investors in the SRI realm, in fact, may and often do invest in companies that support Planned Parenthood and pro-choice alternatives.

2. BRI INVESTS IN COMPANIES THAT ARE RESPONSIBLE FOR SUPPORTING OUR MILITARY EFFORTS, WHILE SRI OFTEN AVOIDS THEM.

Taylor points out that this is often the case, and many that screen for abortion and pro-life issues keep consistency by also screening out companies that make weaponry and support warfare. Again, this does not seem to be a biblical issue for most SRI screeners but a social issue. The exception would be groups such as the Anabaptist community as well as many Catholic organizations who have even gone so far as to screen out the use of Treasury securities because they represent as much as 40 percent of the federal budget for defense. That is biblical for them as the commandment, "You shall not murder (kill) (Exodus 20:13)," is paramount in their thinking.

3. BRI AVOIDS COMPANIES THAT OFFER SAME-SEX BENEFITS WHILE SRI MAY INVEST IN THEM.

Taylor agrees that some SRI screeners do indeed do this.

4. BRI AVOIDS COMPANIES THAT PRODUCE AND SELL PORNOGRAPHY WHILE SRI MAY INVEST IN THEM.

Taylor rightly points out again that some rare SRI screeners may indeed invest in pornography as a freedom of speech issue, but the faith-based SRI participants that she is familiar with are very strongly in the same camp as the BRI providers and have strong screens against the pornography industry.

5. SRI TAKES ACTIVE ROLES IN IMPROVING CORPORATE GOVERNANCE, WHILE BRI MOSTLY IGNORES THAT ISSUE.

6. SRI IS ACTIVELY ENGAGED IN ENVIRONMENTAL ISSUES, WHILE BRI MOSTLY IGNORES THAT ISSUE.

7. BRI advocates investment in adult stem cell research, while SRI invests in almost all forms of stem cell research.

The same exception should be noted as above for issues such as abortion and Planned Parenthood, as many of the same faith-based SRI screeners will break with other SRI investors and screen these items in the same way as BRI investors.

8. BRI AND SRI INVESTORS COMMONLY SCREEN OUT COMPANIES IN THE TOBACCO, ALCOHOL AND GAMING INDUSTRIES.

As much as 50 percent of the issues actually may be screened in a large cap portfolio. This seems obvious, but without a game plan and an understanding of your own personal needs for how BRI could affect you, it is impossible to get off the treadmill of investing just like everyone else. The lessons taught in Romans 14 encourage everyone to be convinced of issues of faith.

Because God works in different ways and on different time-tables with each person, this concept may take time to awaken the passion in each of us. A starting point, however, would be to do an inventory of all the places you have investments and look critically at how each of those pools of money is invested. Let's begin with a listing of plans and accounts:
* Defined contribution plans such as 401(k) or 403(b)
* Individual Retirement Plans such regular IRA, IRA Rollover, Roth IRA, Simple Employee Pension Plan (SEP) or Keogh Plans

- Personal brokerage accounts including custodial accounts
- Corporate retirement plans
- Corporate cash reserves
- Trust funds
- Endowment funds, including long-term funds donated to churches, colleges and schools
- Any pool of funds that contains stocks, bonds or mutual funds

Each of these entities has unique objectives, and if you are responsible for the investment of the funds inside these accounts, then you are carrying an earthly title of owner or trustee. That means that you are responsible for the assets that are held inside those plans and accounts. If you have been relying on an advisor or manager to run these funds, you have transferred some of this responsibility to be shared with others, but, ultimately, you are still the "owner" or "trustee."

If you want to go back to the premise from Chapter 1 that God really owns it all, this also is a good time to reiterate that God also has placed us as Christians in our unique positions to see how we handle the challenge. Investors who were smart enough to save and fund their IRAs and 401(k)s may also have been lucky enough to have lived during the time of a great bull market in stocks such as the U.S. market from 1981 through 2006. Does God care how you got this money and does He care how you will leave a legacy? Our premise is that the answer to both of these questions is clearly YES! Can one advisor or one investor make a difference? YES!

THE DIFFERENCE BRI CAN MAKE

Many of you are aware of the private equity efforts to take the company, First Data Corp (FDC), private. FDC was the centerpiece of a controversy a few years back when it was being screened out by money managers who were trying to avoid companies that were not living up to the standards set by many believers.

The point of contention stemmed around the fact that this company had a great track record and growth trend that was developed from processing credit cards. One of the fastest-growing segments of FDC's business was in the area of pornography. As the awareness of this was growing, one broker discovered that his firm had just placed a buy recommendation on FDC. The broker called the analyst and asked why the analyst would recommend a company that had such a large exposure to porn. The analyst confessed he was not aware of the extent of the exposure to the pornography industry. The rather confused analyst reworked his numbers, and one month later pulled the recommendation.

A little more than a year later, FDC decided to get out of the business of dealing with the porn industry, and the company then became a favorite of several of the same BRI money managers who just one year earlier were thumbs down on it. There is no effort to connect the dots and indicate that FDC changed their corporate strategy because of one pulled analyst rating—but who knows?

How are each of your funds invested and how did they get that way? Did you make the investment decisions or have you delegated the management of the investments to others? The questions for you to ask yourself are different for each situation, but here is the framework that I would suggest you start with if you wish to bring a greater degree of biblical influence to your holdings:

You Make the Decision with Individual Stocks

It is time to start reading the annual reports of the companies in your portfolio if you are making the investment decisions. Then, after reading the annual reports, it is important to complete and vote the proxy forms for each company. Many will scoff at this as it is difficult to think that one vote will make a difference in the world of corporate governance as it exists today. Never forget that one vote here and one vote there could add up to a lot of changes in the way public companies are being run. Stop throwing the proxy in the wastebasket on top of the annual report! Do you realize every time you do, the people who run these companies are free to exercise their will without getting input from the owners... that's you by the way! In case you haven't realized it, those presidents and chairmen of the boards are supposed to work for you!

Take a big-picture view of each company in the portfolio. What is the business of the company? Do you believe that any of their activities would fall into the list of nine deadly sins—we'll get to those in Chapter 5—that Christian money managers weed out when building their portfolios? Do any of the companies in your portfolio, in fact, show an effort to be part of the solution we seek as Christian investors, by conducting themselves in an exemplary way in dealing with the public? You may want to write to the company directly and ask if any of its operations are violating your concerns as a Christian (see Appendix B and Appendix F). You also might purchase research on this subject and compare your portfolio to the information compiled in these pages to help you deal with these issues.

It is just as important, however, to look at what companies are doing right and not to be obsessed with the sins of companies. Too often Christians are seen as only emphasizing the negative, and in many cases this is a legitimate criticism. Part of your overview should include the analysis of whether the companies in your portfolio are doing their part to promote many of the opposite sides of what we list as the nine deadly sins in a later chapter. Consider how your holdings are structured. For example, are there only mutual funds in your holdings or do you have both individual stocks and mutual funds? Here is a way of looking at each situation:

When Money Managers Choose Individual Stocks

When money managers are hired to steward your money, they are engaged because of their history of performance and the system of money management that fits with your objectives and level of risk assumption. If you throw another requirement at them to screen all of their choices based on your Christian worldview and whether the companies fulfill BRI standards, your demand may be met with resistance. Depending on how forceful you and your advisor are in influencing the money manager, many will even require you to sign a separate agreement that indicates you understand that they may not perform as well if you impose additional restrictions such as BRI. If your money manager earns 10 percent for all of his or her other clients and 7 percent for you with BRI restrictions, will you be satisfied with that result? In fact, the opposite case, where the BRI screened portfolio outperforms other clients, is more likely to happen. When that occurs for a few years, money managers usually stop asking you to sign the forms.

The best way to approach this is to sit down with your financial advisor/money manager and explain your concern. If neither of them is able to communicate an adequate solution to this quandary, then it may be time to start shopping for new professionals that can approach this problem with your authority. Even though they are very informed about the markets and individual stocks in their universe, the managers and advisors must work for you to meet your objectives. As a Christian, it is reasonable for you to not want to invest in sinful products or companies that perpetuate lifestyles and attitudes that are counter to your heart and your biblical worldview.

Mutual Funds Which You Manage

The easiest way to find out about your funds that are being held in your accounts is to ask your advisor for summary sheets on each fund that describes the investment strategy and lists the top 10 holdings. This will not only give you a feel for what is being held indirectly for you inside the fund, but it also will give you a chance to see if you are actually diversifying. Frequently you will find your funds often hold many of the same stocks.

The most important document to read about a mutual fund is the prospectus. You likely received one when you purchased the fund, but if you threw that away—as many clients do—then call your fund and get an updated version or just go online and download. Most of the funds have toll-free numbers, and you can order a prospectus without talking to anyone. Be assured, however, it will be a gold-plated rarity if your fund's prospectus mentions anything close to the words Bible or biblical in the strategies of how it invests your money.

It will become more obvious what type of strategy your fund manager is following when you obtain a listing of your fund's top 10 holdings. This is a standard way of sharing the work a manager is doing on behalf of shareholders by giving you an array of companies that make up 20 to 30 percent of your fund's assets. This also will show you the concentration of funds in industry sectors, and this, too, will give you an idea of how the managers are trying to achieve their objectives.

Many Christian financial advisors offer their clients a screening tool that will break down all of the holdings of a mutual fund and list the percentage of each fund's holdings that violate their screens. An example of that screening technique is known as "The Evaluator." As a proprietary system of research it can be an eye opener when it brings out the truth about a fund's holdings.

MUTUAL FUNDS (YOUR ADVISOR CHOOSES YOUR FUNDS)

There is not much different about this scenario compared to the previous one as you must still ask your advisor what the funds will be doing about screening for your interests, even if your advisor chooses for your accounts. As you plug into a system like The

Evaluator, you will still obtain the same information about how a fund's holdings compared with the screening technique being used. Don't be afraid to make your advisor's job a little more difficult, by insisting on having him find what you want, in order to make sure you feel that the funds you end up with, reflect your values and not the professional's.

BONDS AND FIXED-INCOME INVESTMENTS

Exactly the same routine can be used by the issuers of debt instruments because this represents money you as the investor are loaning to each company. You may be enabling a company to do all of the objectionable activities discussed earlier, but you have no vote in the company's direction. Your only vote here is to divest any holding in a company you find in violation of your biblical standards.

This overview of your holdings may be very revealing as to the real activities of the company in your portfolio. A few years ago, while attending a national conference of Christian advisors, I heard many attendees talking about the subtle advertising scheme of a clothing company called Abercrombie and Fitch. Because all of our children were out of college, and my familiarity with this company amounted to hearing loud music when I passed their stores in the mall, it didn't occur to me that they were anything but a very aggressive marketer to teens. Then I learned that they sent out magazines with photographs that bordered on soft porn in slick ads to the kids who signed up at these stores, selling them on the normalcy of this type of lifestyle. The management appeared not to be receptive to any entreaty to clean up this advertising or to discuss the merits of this lifestyle. In more recent years, however, the management has made some efforts at selective listening but still market through very suggestive and liberal images of the ideal lifestyle.

After listening and thinking how blessed I was to be a parent of children in their 30s instead of teens, it was time to check my portfolio. The first holding in the first portfolio I reviewed was none other than Abercrombie and Fitch! I immediately called my money manager, who was surprised by my decision to divest this company and questioned why. After listening to my reasons, my money manager sold my stock the next day. But that's not all: Four weeks later, the same money manager sold his entire position, or all of his clients' Abercrombie and Fitch stock. Had everyone converted to Christianity?

No, they simply became aware that this company was taking liberties with a moral position. Likewise, you also will find some incredibly immoral activities that are being subsidized by the companies in your own portfolio, and you will want to clean it up. The greatest value Christians can be in the world is to be the salt and light that we are called to be!

OTHER VOICES IN THE MARKETPLACE

There are numerous books and studies that are available for investors to read about the SRI activities that have taken place and are still being forged by many different groups. There is very little in print at this time on the BRI approach, but I am confident that it is just a matter of time before that will change. It is easy to think that investors are either SRI or BRI, when, in fact, there are so many instances where it is likely that investors will draw what they want from both disciplines. One of the prolific authors and lecturers on financial matters, who shuns the term "biblical" in his views of implementing an investment strategy, is Gary Moore of Gary Moore & Company. Despite his reticence, his work has been very helpful to those in BRI as a reference for many of the same issues that confront Christians in learning about finance and faith and how they are related.

Often found in forums that deal with SRI issues, he has brought a Christian perspective to the table in that realm. When discussing BRI, he often tries to bring social and mission concerns to the dialogue. His point is that it is possible for all investors to miss the mark if they confine their thinking to one set of values and one group's thoughts.

The point is well taken! Keep reading all you can on this subject and adjust your thinking as new ideas come along that also fit with where the Lord is leading you.

QUESTIONS TO CONSIDER

1. What do you think of the term Biblically Responsible Investing after reading the first few chapters of *Kingdom Gains?*

2. Why do you think Romans 13 and 14 are so important to the concept of BRI?

3. Are you able to compare and contrast the strategies of BRI and SRI? Do you tend to favor one investing style over the other?

4. What is the best way to begin implementing a BRI strategy? Can you do this for yourself? Do you know an advisor who is able to help you to do this?

5. Are you convinced that there are some things in your investments that could be done more along the lines of a BRI strategy? What will you do next to change that?

5

NINE DEADLY SINS:
WHERE DO I DRAW THE LINE?

[Americans are gravitating toward] a religion that is easygoing and experiential rather than rigorous and intellectual...We must fight the temptation to treat our faith the way we treat our careers—as a source of entertainment, fulfillment, and happiness. Remember the warning of C.S. Lewis: If you're seeking happiness, don't choose Christianity, choose port wine.

Chuck Colson

In 1976 I was invited by an elderly gentleman to serve on an investment advisory board for a pool of money related to a religious university. South Africa was under apartheid rule, and someone soon introduced the notion that our funds in the college's endowment should not contain any companies doing business there.

The idea that selling shares of a company in an obscure fund in Northeast Ohio might have an impact on cruel atrocities in an African country, bent on white supremacy, was new to me. This issue would fall under an aspect of corporate governance as the managements of each company would weigh the advantages of conducting business in a place of controversy.

After a great deal of study and research, however, the concept of socially responsible investing started to take shape for me. It was not automatically obvious to me that all companies doing business there were part of the problem. There were, in fact, companies that were providing housing for the South African workers that was far superior to their former residences, but not up to the standards of some of the do-gooders who tried to use every wedge possible to make political gains. It also was important to remember that even in companies that were deemed "guilty" of doing business in a place that furthered apartheid, there were still believers in those companies that were trying to serve God and be a witness where they were called.

As it turns out, even Nelson Mandela, the imprisoned and embattled foe of apartheid, was not in favor of selling the shares of all companies that were doing business in South Africa at the time. He has since stated, that it was the companies who stayed and brought economic pluses in the lives of people, by hiring them when local companies would not hire blacks, that made a difference. Many of these same companies built housing that was adequate and available to employees who otherwise could not have afforded it.

The moral of this story: Look at each company and examine all aspects of its activities to see if it is part of the problem or part of the solution. That is still true of the companies that are viewed in today's marketplace as offenders in the Biblically Responsible Investment world. Because no organization is completely pure any more than another organization is completely offensive, the effort should be made to identify companies that are primarily offering services and products that are counter to the principles that Christians embrace through their biblical worldview. How can we identify these sinful activities that should prompt us to take action?

There could be 10 or 12 deadly sins or many more than that. But in the world of investing, these are the most common areas of concern that money managers focus on in evaluating the activities of a company and in determining whether they are in violation for faith-based investors. If a company is doing great things to improve the world we live in, then that also is part of many valuations. Companies that incur a violation from one screener will sometimes be pardoned by another screener because the violations are not of material concern.

An example of this is a company found to contribute to Planned Parenthood. This is considered a violation by many Christians as Planned Parenthood is one of the largest providers of abortion services. In analyzing company contributions, however, one may learn that the corporation is providing matching grants for employee contributions. Therefore, if one of its employees contributes to Planned Parenthood—or any other charity or non-profit organization—the company honors its pledge to match its employee's philanthropic effort. On the other hand, companies who also send contributions to organizations such as Planned Parenthood from their corporate earnings are, indeed, doing this on behalf of all shareholders in their proportionate ownership. It makes a big difference to a shareholder who realizes that his company is supporting organizations that fund abortions.

In presenting this concept in lectures and meetings to a wide audience, many questions start to come up, such as, "Where do you draw the line"? Or, "What about a bank stock where the bank is loaning money to a beer distributor? What about a cruise ship line that provides gambling on board their ships, but this represents less than 5 percent of company revenues?"

My answer is the same question: Where will you draw the line? As you pray about this issue, God will guide you in what you must do about your investments. You may find that your decision about where to draw the line will differ from others. The important thing it seems to me is to start by drawing the line somewhere!

Deuteronomy 23:17-18 says, *"No Israelite man or woman is to become a shrine prostitute. You must not bring the earnings of a female prostitute or of a male prostitute into the house of the Lord your God to pay any vow, because the Lord your God detests them both."*

This passage indicates that in the fifth book of the Bible, in the early history of mankind, God revealed His desire and told followers that He does indeed care where we get our money!

Think of it this way: Does it make any difference to you that Time Warner makes a practice of profiting on music whose lyrics are utter smut? What if you're a shareholder? Does it change your perspective when you own part of the company?

Let's take this idea to another level: If the profits from this and other entertainment caused the stock to rise, and a shareholder then donated this stock to the church, should the church accept it? Do you see the need to draw the line? *Where will you draw it? Where should the church?* By the way, to solve this particular dilemma many churches and organizations will accept a donation in a company that may not pass its screening, but then will divest the stock as soon as practicable.

There also is valid debate as to whether you should *divest* or *protest* once you determine that there are activities in a company that are in direct violation of biblical principles. When all Christian shareholders divest and sell their interest, who is to remain to be a witness to the management of these companies? When a company's violations are readily apparent and central to their business, divestiture is an easy option. But there may be times when a protest is more suitable. For example, when a company's long-term business and products are not in violation, but other negatives, such as excessive executive compensation or backdating of stock options, exist, then a protest movement might be your best weapon. More than ever, a well-written and well-conceived letter is still one of the best ways of being heard. Corporate executives often will dismiss one or two letters, but when five or 10 or more on the same subject start rolling in that make valid points, corrective action often follows.

Because there will be different interpretation about what constitutes an unacceptable investment, it is important to enter this arena with a spirit of unity, acknowledging that there are many areas that are obviously objectionable and others that will cause debate.

What companies would Jesus own? Companies that are engaged in profiting from the following activities are begging for your scrutiny as to whether God is calling you to divest them from your investments:

1.   TOBACCO

Don't you know that you yourselves are God's temple and that God's Spirit lives in you? 17If anyone destroys God's temple, God will destroy him; for God's temple is sacred, and you are that temple. (1 Corinthians 3:16-17).

- Manufacturers and purveyors of tobacco
- Scientific data has provided conclusive proof of what people already knew: cigarettes slowly damage and kill the bodies of those who smoke. Despite this, smoking in the United States is down only slightly, despite all of the legal efforts to ban smoking in many places. Meanwhile, the tobacco companies have taken their advertising to countries overseas and in developing parts of the world where consumption in many places is at all time highs. It seems like such a no-

brainer that anyone would waste money on such disgustingly filthy products—but it's happening, and Christians are contributing to the problem.

2.   ABORTION

Jesus said, "Let the little children come to me, and do not hinder them; for the kingdom of heaven belongs to such as these" (Matthew 19:14).

"See that you do not look down on one of these little ones. For I tell you that their angels in heaven always see the face of my Father in heaven" (Matthew 18:10-11).

"The God who made the world and everything in it is the Lord of heaven and earth and does not live in temples made by hands. And he is not served by human hands, as if he needed anything, because he himself gives all men life and breath and everything else" (Acts 17:24-25).

Life is a gift from God, and companies that work in the abortion industry are considered unacceptable investments by many Christians. These include:

- Manufacturers of abortion materials
- Hospitals that perform abortions for profit when not required by state laws
- Insurance companies that pay for abortions as a benefit
- Contributors to Planned Parenthood and other agencies supporting abortion
- Researchers who harvest stem cells from aborted children

Without debating if there is ever an abortion that God would approve, I can contend with great certainty that God is pro-life! It is quite apparent to me that our Lord must be in great agony when observing how prevalent this procedure is in our world today. In the United States alone, it is estimated that we have officially killed 50 million babies (pro-choicers would use the term *fetuses*) since the passage of Roe v. Wade. Some point to the fact that the annual number of abortions has dropped to about a million babies as if that is a positive trend. Just thinking about the waste of human talent that we are missing brings tears to the eyes of many people. If any other childhood disease was killing a million infants every year, it would be the primary target for eradicating that disease and that issue would be the centerpiece of every political campaign. The least Christians can do is to check the companies in their portfolios to make sure they are not funding Planned Parenthood or research that is making body parts a centerpiece of the profit margin for their earnings.

3.   PORNOGRAPHY

Do not love the world or anything in the world. If anyone loves the world, the love of the Father is not in him. For everything in the world— the cravings of sinful man, the lust of the eyes and the boasting of what he has and does—comes not from the Father but from the world (1 John 2:15-16).

Who may ascend the hill of the Lord? Who may stand in his holy place? He who has clean hands and a pure heart, who does not lift up his soul to an idol, or swear by what is false (Psalm 24:3-4).

- Producers of "adult" film and music
- Distributors of smut
- Internet providers and content providers emphasizing porn
- Adult entertainment companies
- Credit card companies specializing in porn

The ease of access of this type of material on the Internet has made this one of the most permeating problems for all segments of our society. The Christian church is not immune from this problem as studies have shown this to be as common in the homes of believers as non-believers.

4. ENTERTAINMENT

You used to walk in these ways, in the life you once lived. But now you must rid yourselves of all such things as these: anger, rage, malice, slander, and filthy language from your lips (Colossians 3:7-8).

Therefore, I urge you, brothers, in view of God's mercy, to offer your bodies as living sacrifices, holy and pleasing to God—this is your spiritual act of worship. Do not conform any longer to the pattern of this world, but be transformed by the renewing of your mind. Then you will be able to test and approve what God's will is—his good, pleasing and perfect will (Romans 12: 1-2).

- Anti-family producers and providers
- Anti-family advertisers

The range of media products, including music, movies, television, radio and Internet games, is often just the tip of the iceberg when it comes to how pervasive smut has become in our society. Because someone has to produce the garbage and someone else has to propagate it, there are many places for investors to be on the watch for violations. For example, at the January 2007 meeting of the smut industry's Internext trade show, discussion centered on how to present and charge for on-demand viewing of sexually explicit material, including watching live performers from the privacy of one's hotel room. Meanwhile, Christian groups are searching and scrambling to find hotel chains that have disdained the adult entertainment industry in the room offerings for guests.

5. LIFESTYLES

The look on their faces testifies against them; they parade their sin like Sodom; they do not hide it. Woe to them! They have brought disaster upon themselves. Tell the righteous it will be well with them, for they will enjoy the fruit of their deeds (Isaiah 3:9-10).

- Financial support for the expansion of lesbian, gay, bi-sexual and trans-gender lifestyles, also known under the acronym LGBT or sometimes GLBT

- Employee training that purports the normality of the LGBT agenda
- Active involvement of corporate funds in the advancement of the LGBT agenda

Many of you will be surprised to find that all of these alternative lifestyles have grown to the rank of great importance in the corporate world as these groups seek to establish their credibility in the same way racial and gender differences received attention and action. For example, there are court cases pending which seek to eliminate gender-defined public restrooms because they discriminate against those with sexual variances to the biblical norm of uniquely male and female. Companies find themselves in a great deal of turmoil in interpreting various employment discrimination laws in light of many court tests on these issues. Organizations that refuse to be intimidated by the ACLU and other left-wing protagonists on same-sex benefits are to be applauded and perhaps included in one's portfolio.

6.   ALCOHOL

Wine is a mocker and beer a brawler; whoever is led astray by them is not wise (Proverbs 20:1).

But now I am writing you that you must not associate with anyone who calls himself a brother but is sexually immoral or greedy, an idolater or a slanderer, a drunkard or a swindler. With such a man do not even eat (1 Corinthians 5:11).

- Manufacturers and purveyors of alcohol

The long record of those who have been harmed by addiction to alcohol makes this area of investment hands-off for many Christians. This also is a classic example of why sin stocks appeal to other investors. Some investors appreciate the built-in market buried in the habits of addicts who cannot stop themselves from drinking. Add the subtle ways of advertising aimed at increasingly younger drinkers, and the market keeps growing even though the evils of this product are quite well known.

7. GAMBLING AND GAMING

For this reason God sends them a powerful delusion so that they will believe the lie and so that all will be condemned who have not believed the truth but have delighted in wickedness (2 Thessalonians 11-12).

A greedy man brings trouble to his family, but he who hates bribes will live (Proverbs 15:27).

- Casino and hotel operators who rely on gaming
- Equipment manufacturers who provide gaming items
- Internet specialty companies who promote gaming online

Some of you may identify with people who love to go to Las Vegas or to Atlantic City and look at it like the cost of any vacation. Others who enjoy gambling tell me they never lose, but if that were true, one would not see the incredible buildings and hotels in the gambling Meccas. As the passage in Thessalonians reminds us, the palaces of the gambling casinos is a tribute to the losers, not those who claim to win all the time. The real sin here is the false impression that you can get rich quick or get something for nothing—one that often ensnares. Addiction in this arena is not uncommon either, although the families who suffer from the problem gambler are not as well known as those who suffer from alcohol, drug and smoking addictions.

8. CORPORATE GOVERNANCE

The integrity of the upright guides them, but the unfaithful are destroyed by their duplicity (Proverbs 11:3-4).

Do not be misled: "Bad company corrupts good character." Come back to your senses as you ought, and stop sinning; for there are some who are ignorant of God—I say this to your shame (1 Corinthians 15: 33-34).

- Companies who overpay their executives at the expense of their workers

- Companies who shower stock options on their management with no accountability
- Managements who will not consider the rights of shareholders
- Companies who slide huge compensation packages through the proxies with no financial information on the cost of such packages
- Managements who exclude major parts of the corporate team from decision making
- Companies that forge mergers and restructurings for personal gain

There are too many examples of companies and their management that have turned money-grubbing when given opportunities to sell out, go private, do a leveraged buyout, backdate stock options or stack their compensation committee so that their paychecks look more like the GDP of a medium-sized country than that of a corporation. Here are two illustrations to give you a feel for the gravity of this deception and help you to understand why Christians must be aware of what is happening in their holdings:

THE CASE AGAINST EXECUTIVE EXCESSES

In the latter part of 2006, the management of OSI (Outback Steakhouse) decided that being a public company was not in the best interest of existing shareholders because the stock was stuck in the mud and "all" efforts to get the stock moving had failed. Management conveyed the company position that all efforts and ideas to maximize value for existing shareholders had been exhausted and company management had resolved to "help" out existing shareholders by buying all the stock back from them at $40 per share. This announcement indeed did bring a pop in the stock, which, in fact, was stuck in the mud in the low $30s for some time.

What is ironic is that many of the same people who already had made billions from having founded the company and taken the stock public many years earlier now wanted to buy back all the stock using surprisingly little of their own money to do so.

What didn't come out in the details right away was the fact that these original owners would indeed have a big payday from a transaction that brings more questions than answers as to how this helps the shareholders. The three founders would raise their ownership rights from 10.7 percent at the outset to 15.3 percent after the buyout. They also would be eligible to receive annual paychecks of $6.4 million each and participate in a bonus pool with other top executives. The excuse for this plan was that they would be on the hook for some of the debt that would be created to buy shares back. Who knew, however, if that would be non-recourse debt, where the borrower does not have to pay back the loan if the company goes under, or if they would truly be held re-sponsible if something went wrong? In fact, their debt proceeded to drop in value as the economic conditions following this event affected OSI's business in a negative way.

The private equity firm that was bringing the funding also will not want to hang around for long either. Their plan will include trying to dump the company back on the market in the next three or four years. You will likely see another new issue offering of this same company with a new payday of billions more going to these same investors.

If this is such a good idea for a small band of buyout investors, why not do the same thing for current shareholders—or at least give them a fair value for their shares, which would mean more like $55-57 per share and not $40. In early 2007, investors were balking at this deal so much that OSI postponed the meeting to cast the votes on this deal three times because they couldn't get shareholders to go along with the shell game. The shareholders eventually ran out of time and desire to fight and threw in the towel after a small increase in the price paid to them. The company went private, and insiders pocketed more money in fees. Time will tell if the company survives the credit crunch of this decade to once again go public. Two years after this transaction took place the now private company had sold many assets and was struggling to pay down debt and make ends meet. It may take a little longer than planned to turn this around to their benefit.

This particular topic has many sources of information, but a good summary of the history of abuse on this topic is found in a book by Robert Monks called Corpocracy. His purpose is to challenge investors with the task of reining in the managers of large corporations on the part of shareholders—a task which he indicates is both overdue and quite difficult as most shareholders are quite passive and unconcerned as long as their stock goes up. Come to think of it, shareholders have become passive even if their shares go down.

HOME DEPOT CORPORATION

Look at the case of Home Depot. This summary from the New York Times business page Sunday, December 31, 2006, on Robert Nardelli, CEO of Home Depot, describes the problem:

> The lushly compensated chief executive of Home Depot, who ran the company's annual shareholder meeting like a Gulag chief. No directors appeared, and Home Depot limited questions from its owners to just one per person—and they couldn't last longer than a minute. When a questioner asked about board independence and conflicts of interest, Mr. Nardelli replied: "This is not the forum in which to address these comments." Mr. Nardelli later apologized for the performance. But the damage was done. In late December, an activist shareholder announced plans to propose in 2007 that an independent committee assess

Home Depot management. Stay tuned to see if he'll be forced to make his proposal at the meeting in one minute or less.

Nardelli subsequently resigned after he was pressured by the board to reduce his salary. His parting "gift" from the company was to receive $210 million on top of his previously incredible five years of compensation while shareholders during his tenure achieved a net return of negative 3 percent. All along this way, shareholders voting their proxies with management had given tacit and official approval of this type of management. All who failed to vote their proxy did just as poorly, through their implicit approval.

9.   ENVIRONMENTAL NEGLIGENCE

For everything God created is good, and nothing is to be rejected if it is received with thanksgiving, because it is consecrated by the word of God and prayer (1Timothy 4:4-5).

The earth is the Lord's, and everything in it,, the world, and all who live in it; for he founded it upon the seas and established it upon the waters. Who may ascend the hill of the Lord? Who may stand in his holy place? He who has clean hands and a pure heart, who does not lift up his soul to an idol or swear by what is false (Psalm 24:1-4).

- Companies that pollute the environment
- Companies that ignore the legal structure for preserving the environment
- Managements who make selfish short-term decisions that affect the environment

This is an issue that eludes many Christians for some reason, and it is unclear to me why so little has been done by the current group of BRI providers to address companies that violate the environment. Perhaps there is a delicate balance in evaluating companies in this realm because many very responsible companies

86

work in industries that can be polluters. The oil industry comes to mind, and the work that many in this industry do to avoid problems is still not enough to avoid some incredibly ugly accidents. For example, the spill of the Exxon Valdez tanker wreaked havoc on our environment, and yet, in the aftermath of that spill, ExxonMobil made great strides to show its positive side in the cleanup and in the prevention of future spills. Without responsible people in the companies that extract natural resources for the energy needs of our economy, the environment would be in even worse shape than it is.

BP has compounded the problem by their bungling attempts to balance their short term profit needs against the sound principles of safe extraction methods. Just the right amount of government regulation and oversight will encourage productivity while observing safety and conservation needs. Shareholders can have influence in their company by insisting on being a better steward of God's creation!

That being said, we could do better! The scare tactics in many of the arguments about global warming are still not to be overshadowed by the truth of many changes that are taking place in the way we use the world's resources. The disproportionate consumption of energy, where the U.S. uses up to 25 percent of the world's resources for less than 5 percent of the world's populace, is not a great legacy. Investors also would do well to take note of how their companies are dealing with the environment in their businesses. Conservation and pollution concerns ought to be a believer's concern as we adopt the same responsibilities for stewardship of our Creation as we do for other resources.

AND THEN THERE WERE 10

If there were a 10th deadly sin it would come under the heading of military and the armaments. The reason I have not added this as a 10th deadly sin is because there are believers on both sides of this issue, and, rather than tackle this issue, I would merely point out that there are funds that screen out military contractors in order to avoid all investments related to killing, war and violence. Others have offered funds to investors that are invested in companies that only relate to our country's military and call those "patriot" funds. From a biblical standpoint, one can find many examples of how God orchestrated the war efforts of the Israelites in the Old Testament. One also could argue that Jesus offered a new approach by loving our enemies and brought a new paradigm to this age-old argument as to whether there is such a thing as a just war. I'm not going to tell you where to draw the line on this issue, but you should know what the issue is.

THE LINE IN THE SAND

As you consider what God is calling you to do about your investing habits, it is possible you will find fault with me about the gravity of some of the violations listed. Indeed, levels of concern vary for many investors as they view the professionals who manage money with a focus on how to own only those companies that they believe would be pleasing to God. If we differ on any of these matters, it is important to focus not on our differences but on what the Bible is teaching each of us. *Kingdom Gains* is not intended to provide all the answers regarding which companies to own or which investment company you should choose. It is intended to point you back to Scripture and seek God's answer for you in how He is calling you to invest His money that has been temporarily entrusted to you.

> Investing doesn't simply bring profits to the investor (sometimes it doesn't even do that). It also profits the business in which we have invested. A Christian should avoid investing in any enterprise that makes its profit from people doing what they shouldn't. For example, in most cases I

believe people shouldn't take out a second mortgage on their home. Consequently, for me to invest in high-yield second mortgages would be an attempt to profit from others' poor decisions. I would not feel right doing that.

This excerpt from Randy Alcorn's *Money, Possessions and Eternity* summarizes a very simple concept. Investing your money in the wrong places as the subprime debt fiasco from 2004 to 2007 has illustrated, has an impact, and it should be a matter for all believers to decide where they will draw their line in the sand and say, "This is what I believe, and this is how I believe God wants me to invest the money entrusted to me." If this is that time of decision for you, then committing this to prayer is an important next step:

Heavenly Father, I realize that I have not taken my role of investor of your funds very seriously in consideration of what would be pleasing to you! Forgive me for my selfish desire to be like the rest of the world and only count what profits would do for my lifestyle instead of what it could do for the Kingdom. Help me to be wise and seek good counsel in all of my dealings going forward. Amen.

QUESTIONS TO CONSIDER

1. The Bible teaches us that God does not rank our sins, but that any and all sins will separate us from Him. Despite the fact that God does not rank them, are there some issues that you consider so important that you cannot ignore them, relative to how you invest the funds the Lord has entrusted to you? If so, which ones are they, and why do you feel that way?

2. How do you start to do research on companies to see if they are in violation of any of the sins you find to be objectionable?

3. Where does one draw the line when it comes to sinful activities? Are you comfortable buying a product from a company if you find it doing despicable things? If there is no such thing as a righteous company, why do we bother to try to find things wrong with any of them?

4. What impact can we possibly make by either not investing a few dollars in a company or by not purchasing any of their products? How do I decide whether to stay in a company as an investor and try to be salt and light, versus just selling my shares and getting out?

6

WHERE DO I GO
TO FIND A BRI PROVIDER?

The days when portfolio decisions can be made in a complete
moral and social vacuum are numbered.
The Financial Times

Starting my career at Merrill Lynch offered many advantages, but one of the dubious distinctions was the infamous crude humor that originates in the trading rooms of Wall Street. I'm not trying to make excuses, but I must confess to rare instances when my environment got the best of me, and my witness suffered from my anger and outrage. One of the most embarrassing incidents took place my second year in the business. By this time, I had established a rapport with bond traders and expected fair treatment when buying and selling bonds for my clients. When I discovered that one of my traders was marking up bonds on me and my clients, it infuriated me. When I confronted him on this, and he still denied any wrongdoing, my long suppressed vocabulary of filthy words literally quieted a noisy boardroom of 75 people who heard me go off on this trader. As I slammed the phone down in disgust and anger, my colleagues started clapping as if they were pleased to know I had succumbed to the same emotions they had. Let me point out, however, that they also knew from this day forward that being a Christian did not involve being perfect but requires each of us to deal with the same original sin that is in us all and will creep out when we least want it to.

BE ON THE LOOKOUT FOR SELF DEALING

Unleashing one's storehouse of filthy language is not the only or most common temptation on Wall Street. Brokerage firms are hot-house environments for the temptation to sell things to your clients that might be questionable at best and downright dishonest at the least. This could involve special stock offerings that bring an inflated commission or it could be that the company was in need of special effort by the sales force to help out a failing department that needed to raise capital. Another common tendency is to jump on a moving train when the idea is hot. The best example of this took place in the '90s when technology was the buzzword on the street. If brokers could slap the right technology story onto a stock, voila! It became instantly saleable. Currently, the hottest button is hedge funds, and not all of them are worth the fees being charged. The terminology, "Let's put some lipstick on this pig and move it," had to have started on Wall Street as stockbrokers figured out ways to make sales. Unfortunately, the chance to see pigs with lipstick has not been limited to one-time events, and one of the advantages of working with experienced advisors is the hope that they can recognize the "pigs" and make sure they don't end up in your portfolio. Don't be surprised when some of these hedge funds that are playing fast and loose with other people's money blow up in the next few years.

CHALLENGES FOR THE YOUNG FINANCIAL ADVISOR

After completing the training program at Merrill Lynch, an account executive—as we were known then—was placed in a cubicle and given a pencil, telephone book and, most important, a telephone to start contacting people to recruit clients. This is one of the most humbling periods of a financial advisor's life. Unless you come from a wealthy family who sends all their relatives and friends your way, this involves making 100 calls a day to get five positive responses in order to secure one appointment. After five appointments, you will likely get one new account. This is why it is hard to see just anyone jumping into the financial services business without some contacts. It also is why financial advisors often delegate the actual investment of a client's funds to professional managers. They have a difficult time building and maintaining their business, much less managing their client's funds. These professionals usually fall into two categories: mutual funds or separate accounts (including hedge funds). Trying to find providers of BRI services for all of the categories of financial assets is a major challenge.

THE MOST POPULAR PLACE—MUTUAL FUNDS

Many of you have already placed your financial success in the hands of a Fidelity Fund, a Vanguard Fund, a Blackrock Fund, an American Fund, an Oppenheimer Fund or one of 20,000 mutual funds that exist in today's marketplace. These fund companies have multiple mutual funds that can meet almost any objective you have as an investor. Others will have passed on mutual funds and hired their own money managers, also known as separate account managers, who invest on one's behalf and charge a fee for that service. By the way, the mutual funds also charge a fee for doing this service, and it is possible to also pay a fee to your advisor for helping you choose which funds to hold. That is how everyone makes their living on Wall Street...finding a way to charge a fee and keep doing it ad infinitum. This also is how an advisor earns his or her keep—by making sure that they add value to pay for these fees.

Notice the word almost in the previous paragraph. If you wanted to call Fidelity or any of the other fund managers listed above and ask for a fund that screens its investments for biblical characteristics, there most likely would not be such a fund. Many would offer "social screens," and a true sign of maturity for the BRI movement will be when secular organizations recognize the need for funds that consider biblical issues before purchasing their holdings. My prayer is that the following words will not be true by the time you read this book: Right now, none of the major mutual funds have any demand to create a fund for Biblically Responsible Investing. That's because investors and advisors have not pounded on the desk demanding such a fund! One thing about Wall Street, if there is a market for anything, it will respond with a product to fill it. As I was writing Kingdom Gains, some of the fund families listed here actually started talking about offering funds with a BRI screen. How great it would be if they beat me to the marketplace by having such a fund before this book is published! By the way, this is how change takes place on Wall Street: if enough people want to own shares in companies that conform to biblical standards, then sooner or later the market will provide products to fill that need.

THE SQUEAKY BRI WHEEL GETS THE GREASE!

What can investors and advisors do now? They can make choices from several providers of BRI services and work with their advisors to start screening for biblical purposes, starting with money managers who don't really want to do it. No matter the inclinations of others, it is God's money you are entrusted with, and if a money manager is unwilling to help you screen unwanted holdings, find a new manager!

Investors who demanded Socially Responsible Investments have been rewarded by seeing so many providers convert to their way of thinking that it is now estimated that 10 to 13 percent of all assets fall under SRI screens. Meanwhile, BRI screening accounts for about 1 percent of all investment assets. Investors must demand choices that include BRI-screened alternatives if the industry is to reach critical mass and become a credible alternative.

There are many people who are involved in making their investments more responsive to biblical teaching, but the professionals who are totally sold out to this purpose are quite small in number and remain very fragmented. Mark Henry, an attorney and Christian Financial Advisor from Carefree, Arizona has suggested that it would be a great idea to have an independent agency that would encourage members to join together to explain biblical screening techniques to the public. This same agency could develop standards for biblical screening and bring out an index that could be useable by investors and money managers, alike, to offer standards of performance, as well.

This does not exist yet, but it is one of the trends to follow in the next few years, as more people demand BRI screening, and the money managers and mutual funds who are offering their services yearn for greater visibility. Until that day when more data exists about money managers and their peer comparisons, each investor is urged to spend time checking out the work being done by all of the providers reviewed in these pages. It is important to repeat—and this will be stated in more than one place in this book—that the presence of any provider in this book is not an endorsement, nor is it a recommendation for anyone to use the companies listed in this chapter. It is our prayer that you look into each of the providers to see if they might fit with how you may wish to invest some or all of your funds. This also is the time to remind you that past performance does not guarantee future results for any of these or any money managers.

THE TIMOTHY PLAN MUTUAL FUNDS

Art Ally spent many years working for traditional Wall Street firms and thought about how he might someday combine his faith with his occupation. That opportunity presented itself in a strange way when a friend who was a pastor at a nondenominational church asked for help in providing investments for its retirement plans. After an exhaustive search trying to find investment choices that would satisfy God's calling toward biblical stewardship, Art discovered that there were no real choices in the mutual fund industry that he could recommend. As he looked more deeply into the holdings of both mutual fund companies and denominational retirement funds, he discovered many companies that were prominent in providing pornography, companies providing services to fund abortions, companies promoting anti-Christian entertainment and companies peddling many other sinful products that were in direct contradiction to the worldview of the pastors that were planning to invest their retirement funds. Art felt God must be calling someone to do something about this but wasn't quite sure he was the one.

He decided to seek the counsel of a friend, CPA Percy Bell. Over lunch Percy challenged Art to make the move. This "move" led Art to start The Timothy Plan of mutual funds and to develop screening techniques that would eliminate these distasteful companies. He was excited to think that the pastors he was called to serve and other Christian investors would now have a choice that would be different from the world. As he contemplated such a fund family, he started to envision how this could touch advisors and investors as well as people in the church, and during the late '80s and '90s, Art's vision came into being.

THE IMPORTANCE OF ENCOURAGEMENT

1Timothy 5:22, along with other passages in Timothy, became the inspiration for Art's wife Bonnie, who became excited about the possibilities that a fund like this could bring to investors. She urged Art to follow his heart and the Lord's calling to start the new fund and call it The Timothy Plan. In April 1994, The Timothy Plan was started, and it has been the launching pad for all of the ministry of Art and Bonnie Ally. Moving from being a successful financial advisor to starting a mutual fund from scratch was a giant leap both financially and spiritually. Many people told Art this was a great idea and indicated support. These same people disappeared from view when the fund was being born and actually started operating. Excuses abounded—everything from political correctness and high risk to being afraid to step out in the marketplace. But Art pressed on because he believed that God was moving in the hearts of many people to help raise funds to start this project. Encouragement from people like Adrian Rogers and many business and venture capital investors who had a Christian worldview kept fueling the startup flames that almost burned out at four distinct times in the birthing process. During those four times, the money had all but dried up in their operation, and the handful of employees of The Timothy Plan started refreshing their resumes as a preface to looking for a job.

GETTING THE MESSAGE TO THE MARKETPLACE

Running out of money was not the only problem in starting a fund family like this. The performances of brand new funds like The Timothy Plan Funds were competing with funds that had larger capital bases and longer track records. Simply put, the early comparisons were not very good. How could they impress financial advisors and Christian investors with the importance of BRI and give funds like Timothy a chance to gain critical mass?

Along came the birthing of the National Association of Christian Financial Consultants, which brought Christian advisors together to share issues of all sorts about their work environments and their need for BRI services. Members of NACFC were eager to recommend The Timothy Plan to their clients, but they often were reluctant to show only a single fund family in deference to traditional concerns about diversification and performance. These issues started to resolve themselves as time passed, the performance of the funds improved, and the choices of funds within the family expanded.

In the first quarter of 2008, The Timothy Plan had eight different funds and has been entrusted with more than $650 million in assets from investors of all walks of life. The Timothy Plan is offered through both large and small investment firms—but not all organizations have established a selling agreement to make the funds available. Investors will have to check with their advisors and custodians to see if Timothy is included in their fund offerings. The screening techniques include monitoring portfolios for the following issues:

1. Abortion
2. Pornography
3. Entertainment (adult and youth)
4. Lifestyles
5. Alcohol
6. Tobacco
7. Gambling

Investors are encouraged to seek information on the fund offerings at www.timothy.com (see Appendix C for more information). The Timothy Plan today employs 15 people who work in marketing and screening to maintain the integrity of the funds' holdings. The actual investments are run by portfolio managers through sub-accounts who follow the dictates of the Timothy screening process.

SEPARATE ACCOUNTS

In addition to mutual funds, financial advisors and investors also can hire a third-party professional manager to work for their clients through a system known as "separate accounts." Clients in this category often will find much higher minimums—$100,000 or more. In a separate-account relationship, the money manager purchases individual stocks and bonds and tries to invest each client's funds according to his or her stated objectives. It is possible that an investor can request any money manager offering separate accounts to deliver BRI type service. Many of the managers will be reluctant to agree to this relationship as they do not analyze companies in this way.

In the mutual fund, the investor actually owns shares of the "fund," whereas the separate-account relationship involves direct ownership. The result is the same when it comes to a Christian who is investing funds and is a fractional owner in all of the companies in either the mutual fund or the separate account. One of the pioneers and leaders in BRI separate-accounts money management is Stewardship Partners.

STEWARDSHIP PARTNERS

Rusty Leonard was one of the top-ranked analysts and money managers for Templeton Investment Management, later known as the Franklin Templeton Group. His tenure included significant responsibility for assets accumulated from the renowned John Templeton, and Rusty often earned Sir John's highest accolades for his work. Rusty always adopted a strategy that avoided placing funds in companies that he thought were destructive to humankind, but it was not formulated specifically to reflect a biblical witness in his early days at Templeton. Ten years of a rewarding career at Templeton were followed by an interlude from the financial wars to set up Wall Watchers and write numerous articles on the non-profit industry. Concerned that the stock market had overheated in the '90's, Rusty wanted to offer Christian investors a choice that would reflect their values, so he acquired an organization known as Biblically Responsible Investing Institute. In April 2001, Rusty began business under the Stewardship Partners banner with the goal of becoming the premier Christian investment management company. His ultimate goal was to see more success for investors followed by greater contributions to worthy Kingdom causes.

OFFERING INVESTORS A CHRISTIAN WORLDVIEW

Investors can hire Stewardship Partners to build individual stock and bond portfolios, and the investments will reflect a view that is quite different from the secular world's way of managing money. From the company's own literature, here is how it describes dealing with these issues:

1. Justice and mercy for the defenseless:
   A. Abortion
   B. Persecution of Christians and other oppressed peoples
2. Justice and mercy for the poor and needy:
   A. Discrimination
   B. Substandard labor practices
   C. Any abuses of the poor, children and the elderly
3. Compassion for those addicted/engaged in sinful lifestyles and those organizations that support such activities:
   A. Alcohol
   B. Gambling
   C. Tobacco
   D. Pornography
   E. Homosexuality
4. Protection of the institution of marriage and the family:
   A. Entertainment that seeks to destroy appropriate attitudes
   B. Efforts to promote alternative lifestyles

Stewardship Partners also has a strong interest in favoring positive behavior so when countries and companies are part of the
solution instead of the problem, it will examine that aspect as
well. For those entities that embrace this point of view:

1. Countries
   A. Personal, political and religious freedom through de-
      mocracy
   B. Economic freedom through capitalism
   C. Fiscal responsibility in government finances
   D. Support for the Jewish people and the state of Israel
2. Corporations
   A. Support for traditional Judeo/Christian values
      Honesty
      Compassion
      Diligence
      Prudence
      Creativity
   B. Support for quality products at fair prices and construc-
      tive stakeholder relations
   C. Support for a sustainable and healthy environment
   D. Support for charitable giving

After compiling all of its own data, an effort is made to gain
insight from other providers of research in this small but growing field. American Values Investments is regularly consulted to
identify companies doing positive things. Investors can find information on its services at www.stewardshippartners.com, and
Appendix C provides other contact information. Not all investment firms are prepared to accommodate setting up accounts
with Stewardship Partners so checking with your financial advisor
will tell you if the company is available in your investment firm's
system. By early 2010, the company had well over $250 million in
client assets which it was investing, as well as eight full-time employees, including three people who have their CFA (Chartered

Financial Analyst) designation and one CPA (Certified Public Accountant) on staff. Their assets have fluctuated significantly during the market volatility of 2008 and 2009. As with most money managers, they experienced challenging times during the down trend of 2008 and almost reversed that with their recovery in 2009. Because they are predominantly an equity manager, their performance is, by definition, more volatile than an investor who measures their performance based on a more diversified group of assets that would often include bonds and alternatives.

Reaching this level of funding after such a short period of time has taught Rusty and his wife a lot about how to trust God. Knowing that he could return to a million-dollar annual salary in the secular world would tempt the patience of most people, but Rusty believes this is where the Lord has called him, and the cost of building an organization is part of that trust. He also trusts that when more Christian investors become aware of the differences in the investment of secular funds compared to a BRI approach, all of the providers in this industry will see tremendous growth. So far, Stewardship Partners has provided investors excellent performance and, in most periods, outpaced their benchmarks as well as provided a bonus above many of the major indexes. As we will point out in Chapter 7, it is important to avoid obsessive number crunching as the performance issue can be distorted by choosing convenient time periods to make a case for or against a manager. Most clients of BRI management have not suffered from underperformance.

AVE MARIA MUTUAL FUNDS

This mutual fund group began business in 2001 with the encouragement and financial backing of several prominent individuals. The man who started Domino's Pizza, Tom Monaghan, was one of the leaders in placing a high priority on changing the culture of Wall Street by offering Catholics and all Christians an alternative to the standard mutual funds. Former Commissioner of Major League Baseball Bowie Kuhn also was an early enthusiast in forming Ave Maria and served on its advisory board for many years. Another key player was George Schwartz from Schwartz Investment Counsel. Schwartz was in the investment advisory business and had built a successful practice by establishing moral guidelines in his strategy. The organizer's vision was to offer all investors, regardless of the size of one's portfolio, an alternative to investing that would avoid companies that were engaging in practices that were sinful in the eyes of Christians.

There are just four areas to remember in the process that Ave Maria uses in screening companies for their portfolios:

1. Abortion
2. Pornography
3. Contributions to Planned Parenthood
4. Non-marital partner benefits

The fund family has six different kinds of funds to meet investors' needs, and even the bond funds and the money market funds must follow the same criteria. If you were to look at the Russell 3000 (trademark) index as an example of a large capitalization listing of companies, the Ave Maria funds would normally screen out about 400 of them. The notion that if you start to screen like this that it will eliminate almost all the companies turns out to not be true at all. In fact, Ave Maria's work has shown that when investing in these types of companies, less than 15 percent are eliminated, and 85 percent are eligible for their funds.

Ave Maria Funds have achieved a significant level of acceptance among investors and rating agencies alike as three of their funds have been rated four out of five stars by Morningstar Rating (trademark) service. The fund group as a whole has accumulated more than $750 million in assets from investors and continues to expand the selling agreements with broker dealers to offer their funds to more people. Interested parties can get more information by going online to their website at www.avemariafunds.com.

Although Ave Maria's original outreach was to Catholic families, Christians from all denominations have become shareholders as they consider the choices available and the issues at hand.

CAMCO INVESTORS FUND AND CORNERSTONE ASSET MANAGEMENT

CAMCO stands for Cornerstone Asset Management Company and has been in existence for quite some time. The company began as a separate accounts money manager in 1984 with an emphasis on morally- and ethically-based investing. The company still has that service, but it added a mutual fund in 2002 called the CAMCO Investors Fund. Because its orientation has been to invest in a morally and ethical way from the outset, you could say that CAMCO was a pioneer in offering this to the marketplace before the concept of BRI came into popularity. It fills a niche for investors who wish to have an equity exposure and want to build wealth with a portfolio that matches its biblical principles. Founder and President Paul Burkhouse built the company by avoiding companies that are principally involved in:

- Tobacco
- Gambling
- Pornography
- Alcoholic beverages
- Abortion

You can find information about the fund at www.camcofunds.com. It should be noted that this fund is not registered in all 50 states so possible investors will need to check carefully to see if it is available. The fund itself is not offered through broker dealers as it is a fund that must be purchased directly from CAMCO. Current assets are less than $20 million. Portfolio manager Rick Weitz indicated that the investors and shareholders in their funds have performed in line with and slightly better than traditional indexes. The normal benchmarking of an appropriate index to compare fund results has not been developed, but the fund managers report many different indexes as the funds invest across many types of companies and styles. In 2007 and 2008, the fund achieved top rankings with one of the periods showing them as the number two fund out of 200.

AMERICAN VALUES INVESTMENT

This fee-only investment advisory firm specializes in "values-driven investing." This is the firm's term for investing in such a way as to find companies that espouse and incorporate positive values in their structure and in their products. After incorporating in 1996, it has developed an investment strategy and systems built around the idea of buying stocks in companies that are doing the right things. Its process awards points based on how companies stack up when rating their history relative to four main values. This is quite distinctive as most managers have their starting point of evaluation built around traditional fundamentals like earnings, dividends and balance sheet fitness. Imagine that you look at a company's track record first in the areas of Integrity, Humility, Diligence and Caring. Only after scoring in the top 25th percentile on these four issues does AVI consider adding an issue to its portfolios. This bias toward finding companies doing positive things is the passion of Carter LeCraw, CEO, and George Parks, vice president.

American Values does not have a mutual fund available for investors at the time of the writing of this book, but it is part of its long-term plan to develop one. They are primarily running separate accounts for their clients, and performance numbers have been very competitive as they have exceeded their benchmarks in most periods. American Values' track record in investing in this manner is supported by several studies that show positive relationships between a stock's price performance and the underlying company's positive values. The firm is currently managing just under $60 million and has been growing steadily. Its primary benchmark is the S&P 500 Index.

FAITHSHARES, INC ETFS

Another important step toward credibility in the marketplace for BRI investments was the introduction of faith based Exchange Traded Funds (ETFs) by an organization called FaithShares, Inc. In December of 2009, they introduced five new ETF's that are screened for specific purposes related to Christian investor's needs. The funds currently available are:

- Christian Values Fund
- Baptist Values Fund
- Lutheran Values Fund
- Methodist Values Fund
- Catholic Values Fund

An ETF combines the diversification of a mutual fund with the liquidity and convenience of an individual stock. The ETF then can be bought and sold just like any individual stock on an exchange while providing both diversification and screening to reflect specific objectives. Investors need to investigate if these funds reflect their interests sufficiently to merit their retention and if they are available thru your advisor. More ETF's are likely to appear in the future as this is an important component in the marketplace.

Almost unnoticed at the time of FaithShares introduction of ETFs, is the attempt to establish an index that could be used as a guideline for BRI comparisons. An organization known as KLD Advisors helps to do the screening for various investment organizations, and along with FaithShares, Inc. they have established the FTSE KLD Christian Values Index. This is intended to properly compare to the Standard & Poor's 500 Index and start to give more traction to the efforts to properly benchmark BRI providers as well as give credibility to the participants in the BRI sphere. All signs of positive movement toward a maturing movement in the marketplace. More information can be found on their website at www.faithshares.com

THE STEWARD FUNDS

This fund group was founded in October 2004, and long-term comparisons are not available at this time. Its strategy is to build optimized portfolios under Modern Portfolio Theory (MPT) and then go backward to screen out issues that do not conform to their Christian worldview. Its strategy attempts to be consistent with biblical principles and a Christian lifestyle. The fund uses Steward Fund Consultants to provide screening information to determine issues that will not fulfill its objectives. Steward's fund is a multiple-asset class fund, meaning it invests in stocks from many different categories, including small, medium and large cap companies. As such, investors need to compare performance against funds and indexes that reflect those same types of stocks. That also makes comparisons more difficult, and investors will find more information at www.StewardMutualFunds.com. A BRI index for the fund(s) would be helpful in making a proper benchmark. Limited performance data on its All Cap Equity Fund is available in Appendix D.

GUIDESTONE FUNDS

This is one of the largest fund providers of screened funds for Christian investors. The fund manager also offers index funds that screen for BRI purposes. The 17 funds with 13 different objectives offer the widest range of investment alternatives. According to its website, "The funds do not invest in any company that is publicly recognized, as determined by GuideStone Financial Resources, as being involved in the liquor, tobacco, gambling, pornography or abortion industries or any company whose products, services or activities are publicly recognized as being incompatible with the moral and ethical posture of GuideStone." Its strategy involves hiring institutional managers to run the money while it monitors the screening process. Investors can view GuideStone's website at www.guidestonefunds.org and also find prospectus and performance information, as well.

The biggest drawback to this manager of almost $10 billion in assets is that it is the new face of the Southern Baptist Annuity Board that offers its services only to members and indirectly to member churches through their state foundations. There is some controversy about the thoroughness of their screenings when compared with other BRI providers. Nonetheless, they have been working to screen securities to the best of their information, for a very long time, and have much experience in this arena.

This organization has one fund that could be very strategic to the entire BRI industry if there was ever a unification effort. GuideStone has had an S&P 500 index fund, but it was still screened for the various issues that did not meet their investment criteria. Because the performance of this fund has been recorded and monitored for many years, it could be the basis for starting a BRI benchmark and, joined with other screening techniques that have been employed since the late 1990s, to build a credible benchmark.

MMA PRAXIS FUND (PRAXIS FUNDS)

This fund group has been in the market place for many years and has served as an investment tool for many religious groups who would call themselves Anabaptists. Origins of the Praxis Funds actually are from the Mennonite tradition, and many of their screening strategies follow along the lines of other BRI funds. Leadership of the Praxis Funds have preferred the term Socially Responsible Investing as opposed to BRI even though many of their screening ideals are similar. This fund family has a large platform of funds available, and investors can use the fund family for a wide diversification of investment objectives. MMA stands for Mennonite Mutual Aid, and it carries a tradition of helping others and being ready to share with those less fortunate, both in our country, and throughout the world.

In actuality, this fund group has been doing more screening based on a "Biblical World View" than any BRI provider. Its desire in communicating with investors is to turn the volume down on labels and stand on their record of focusing on issues that Christians from all walks of life would call important. The organization began just after World War II, and its mutual funds have been operating since 1977. The organization recently made a name change to Everence but their mutual funds will still be known as the Praxis Funds to symbolize their hope for eternal values for their clients.

Screening strategies include positive and negative screens, such as:

1. Alcohol (negative)
2. Gambling and gaming (negative)
3. Pornography (negative)
4. Military and armaments (negative)
5. Corporate governance (positive)
6. Environmental care (positive)
7. Community involvement (positive)
8. Concern for minority stakeholders (positive)

Investors can view all of the funds and the historical performance at its website www.mmapraxis.com.

BRIDGE PORTFOLIO

Another strategy that has emerged to help investors build a BRI portfolio is to allow investors to take the best screening strategies and then build their own portfolios with individual stocks. This may involve more risk than having a professional manager running the money, but for many investors and advisors, this is still a popular choice. To help with the quantitative burden this brings, several providers have started to offer their expertise in this area. One such company is known as Bridge Portfolio, and it now provides portfolio modeling that supports BRI strategies from its offices in Chicago, Illinois. Investors and their advisors can contact them via the web at www.bridgeportfolio.com.

STEWARDSHIP ASSET MANAGEMENT MMA PORTFOLIOS

One of the most recent attempts to make BRI more available to more investors is known as the Stewardship Asset Managers (SAM) life style funds. This is an attempt to roll many of the previously mentioned providers of BRI services into a fund of funds that will be invested with screening techniques based on the needs of each investor. For example, a conservative investor might wish to have 80 percent in bonds and 20 percent in stocks, while a more aggressive person would reverse that allocation. Having the ability to use many managers and control the risk parameters is a popular way for investors to achieve many goals at once.

Because this requires a new format to bring this product to the marketplace, it is too soon to predict the success or performance of this methodology. It does appear however, to be a step in the right direction, as it shows unity among the providers to work together, and it combines what many investors would like to see by being able to access many BRI providers through one investment vehicle. The six money managers, who all are using the BRI Institute's research, are:

- Stewardship Partners (Intl & large cap equities)
- Foundation Financial, Inc. (equities)
- Aletheia Investors (large cap value equities)
- Fred Alger Management, Inc. (mid cap equities)
- The London Company Investors, Inc. (small cap equities)
- Vanguard Intermediate US Treasury Fund (fixed income component)

The objectives of individual investors are met through a series of lifestyle fund choices that are built around six different allocations that start with a very small percentage invested in stocks for the most conservative investor and building up to 80 percent invested in stocks for the most aggressive investor. This type of choice will likely show up in many different ways for investors as this is one of the more popular and economically viable investment alternatives for people. People can choose these both as a startup investment and also for helping people manage their holdings as their needs and objectives change over a lifetime. Investors can contact this group at www.stewardshipassetmanagement.com.

ARIS CORPORATION AND ARIS INVESTMENT SERVICES

Aris is one of the first large, secular investment companies to see the value of offering a faith-based investment platform that addresses the needs of the Evangelical Christian Investor. Aris has devised a system that includes many of the aforementioned providers in a fund of funds that brings a more diversified approach to the concept of BRI investing. This is considered a significant breakthrough for many advisors who feel that they are not able to diversify their clients properly and still achieve the goals of Biblically Responsible Investing.

Part of the company's vision statement is: "We have grown our business based on our Christian values, but our introduction and association with Kingdom Advisors has moved us individually and as an organization to serve financial advisors to increase their ability to create Kingdom Impact with their clients." This means that its focus is more as a wholesaler of investment services and would be most easily accessed through an investment advisor. Aris also has an institutional division so that larger investors could still go directly to them for faith-based investment services.

111

At the time of this writing, performance numbers were not available for a long enough time period to be useful but access to the company's services can be viewed online at www.ariscorporation.com.

THE BEST OF THE REST

You will see names such as Amana Funds (based on the Koran), New Covenant Funds (based on more of a social agenda), Thrivent Funds (formerly known as the Lutheran Brotherhood group of funds) who do no screening at all, along with various funds that are part of variable annuity offerings. Investors are advised to always do thorough research about what each of these investments is attempting to accomplish. There will also be new fund groups sprouting up in the coming years that will offer a BRI approach. One such group is the Eventide Funds, which has received many accolades in the short period of time since its startup. Their presence, and many others that will be coming in the market, will be an answer to prayer, as long as they are staffed with credible investment professionals, and offer a market niche for believers. For a more complete guide to checking out the providers of BRI services, see all the contact information provided in Appendix C.

Many other examples of BRI exist in the market but are often part of a fragmented portion of services that are being done in a management firm that does not offer its services to the general public. Many references have been made about how this concept is one of the fastest growing movements today. That is true, but it still remains a very tiny part of the total volume of all money managers

Readers might wonder about fund families such as Thrivent, which is the new name for funds offered from the Lutheran Brotherhood tradition. Surprisingly, Thrivent takes the position that they have a fiduciary responsibility that supersedes its ability to screen for moral, ethical or biblical purposes. That is why it is so important to check more deeply into all of the funds in a port-folio all the time as even some of the funds we discuss in these pages may change their strategies since this has been written.

There are countless numbers of managers who are trying to provide BRI services today because the investors they work for have asked them to invest that way. As a financial advisor from 2001 until retirement in 2005, I worked with several separate ac-count managers who were willing to help us screen for BRI. . Even since that time, we have found many traditional managers who will help us screen for BRI issues for our foundation. This may be done by many more investors and advisors if the demand is there. It must mean enough to the clients and to Christian ad-visors to provide the service. Wall Street firms will sell anything that the market demands. Clients and advisors, alike, have been too passive about this, and, consequently, we have only a trickle going in this movement right now. But that does not discourage me, and it should not discourage others! Now is the best time to start doing something about it, and we will give you more specific ideas in Chapter 8 about what to do next.

The best thing that could happen for these pioneers in the BRI industry is for them to have 10 more competitors who are offering BRI services. That would continue to validate the growth and also the demand from investors. It also would lead to having the same credibility as the Socially Responsible Investing groups. Corpora-tions will listen more closely when you represent 10 or 15 percent of their shareholders instead of just 1 or 2 percent!

The problem with convincing money managers to provide BRI screening is that they will not have the same mindset in trying to accomplish this if they do not share the faith. Their enthusiasm for eliminating an investment that they are fond of will always carry a dark shadow of performance concern. That is, they want you to know that if they cannot invest in stock A, B or C that the performance could suffer, and this will make them look bad.

Once you decide to invest as a BRI advocate, how do you check on your progress and performance? Has the BRI industry developed performance measurement tools to help investors with this question and make it simple to find out their results?

Would you accept a performance in your investments that is less than the indexes? How much of a performance discount would you be willing to assume to know that you are not investing in areas that would displease God? More importantly, do you have to assume that you will suffer a setback in performance if you invest in a BRI kind of way?

Don't let these and other questions nag at you. Go with me into the next chapter on performance and rate of return compared with non-screened investments. You have more to learn to get started in BRI—including some information that I'm sure you'll consider good news.

QUESTIONS TO CONSIDER

1. How can you tell whether the providers of BRI services perform any better than you would do on your own?

2. Where do you begin to educate yourself on what all of these providers do? Can all brokers do business with all of these providers? What if you wish to have one of these providers added to the list of company choices for your retirement plan? How does one contact them to see if we can use them as providers?

3. What character traits should one consider when choosing an advisor and provider of investment services?

4. Why is it important to try to find investment professionals who share your world view?

7

How Much Will This Cost Me?

If Jabez had worked on Wall Street, he might have prayed,
"Lord, increase the value of my investment portfolios."
Bruce Wilkinson *The Prayer of Jabez*

Several years ago I was helping a client to restructure his investment management team and tried to make certain that all the
managers were doing their part. As often happens in a public
endowment/non-profit investment situation, the managers who
"win" the beauty contests to manage money for the institutions
are often tied to some of the large donors to those same institutions. For example, if you look at the local hospital's endowment
fund, chances are the person receiving investment fees from the
hospital's fund will often be related to someone on the board of
the hospital. You can substitute the word *college* or *church* or *pension fund* for hospital, and you can imagine how the political web

will compete against objectivity when it comes to money management.

After interviewing and processing several managers and narrowing the process to the final choices, along came a last-minute candidate for us to consider. This manager was referred to us by one of the school's large donors. The donor had been using this manager as one of his personal investment managers and recommended him highly as he had been beating the averages. The manager turned out to be a maverick, and this spokesman stated that they had beaten the S&P 500 for the past 10 years. In short, he couldn't imagine a time that they wouldn't beat it year in and year out. Just listening to this guy made me suspicious and reminded me of a statement a client made to me when I met him for the first time. "I hope you are not an expert," he said, "because I have lost more money at the hands of experts and gunslingers than any other source."

CHOOSING AN APPROPRIATE BENCHMARK

I suggested we do more due diligence on this money manager, but the committee was enthralled with the performance and style of this group so they allocated some funds to them despite my reticence. It was soon after this that I saw how they were beating the S&P 500: More than half the portfolio was invested in European and foreign securities, which were doing much better than the domestic indexes at that time. My suggestion to the money manager was that they were using the wrong benchmark, or index used for performance comparisons, and they should be comparing their performance to an index that also carries stocks like the ones in which they were invested. That idea didn't resonate at all with them as they were happy to use the hot stocks of the day to pad their performance and then compare themselves to another index. It was not long before the domestic stock market started outperforming the international markets, making this manager look very bad. In fact, he was fired a few years later. It also points out that wealthy investors are not always the smartest investors.

THE POWER IN ONE NUMBER!

Performance is one of the most elusive and confusing factors for investors to ferret out of Wall Street. The brokerage firms are reluctant to calculate it because it will often be used for the wrong reasons, and the clients are often not able to understand the real meaning of the calculation. Many times in my dealing with clients they will sit and listen for a bit and then they say, "Just give me the one number!" What was my rate of return for last year? What has been my return since we started working together? Well, that's two numbers—but you get the point. By the time we explain the meaning of time-weighted rate of return and dollar-weighted rate of return, most client's brains have turned to mush, and they are begging to just go to lunch or talk about something else. The reason this calculation is so complex is that almost all of our clients are moving money into or taking money out of their accounts. This requires a consideration of how that affects the management and performance of the account.

As a consumer of financial services, the best single one-number question you can ask your advisor is, "What was my time-weighted rate of return for last year?" This number can be skewed at times, but it is most likely that you will get your best comparisons over time if you just use this one measurement.

Furthermore, it also will allow you to choose benchmarks that are stated for the most part in the same way. If your mutual fund is investing in the United States in large companies, then the Dow Jones Industrial Average of 30 industrial companies, the Standard and Poor's 500 Index of the 500 largest companies or the Russell 1000 Index, which is the largest 1,000 companies, could all be possible benchmarks. I promised to not get too technical about this, but for your funds that invest in other segments of the market you will need to find benchmarks that give you an idea of how they stack up against comparable indexes.

This leads us back to the question that is always lurking in the minds of investors who are Christians and want to do the right thing. This revolutionary idea gets the wheels turning right away and provokes the critical question: How much will it cost me? That is, should I pay more for someone to do the screening necessary to help "clean up" my portfolio and then earn less in returns? And, probably more importantly, will my new investment results be as good as my index fund or my advisor's group of managers that I have now?

I DON'T CARE ABOUT PERFORMANCE—UNTIL IT COSTS ME!

Performance is one of three issues. If you shift all of your investments to follow BRI patterns one of three things will happen:

You will attain superior performance.

You will match the same performance as if you were in a secular portfolio.

5. You will receive a lower return than if you were in a secular portfolio.

Because most of you will not have a problem with the first or second, let's assume most of your concern during this chapter will be in dealing with the third event.

Suppose you felt God's calling in this, and it was obvious that the investments you were holding were indeed more in line with your Christian worldview, but those companies were not doing well during this phase of the market. If the indexes were performing at 10 percent and you were earning 8 or 9 percent, would you still believe that it would be more important to go back to owning companies that would be offensive to God? Every investment strategy other than indexing will have this variance from the norm during some stretch of their investment history. Even when you are doing God's will, the performance of your investments will not always carry a superior return in a secular sense. But there is good news!

History Suggests That You Actually Will do Better!

Mary King is a financial advisor with Merrill Lynch in Hollywood, California and has studied and written much on the performance of various portfolios that have used socially responsible and morally responsible screenings. She has written several scholarly (see Appendix D) and public articles on her findings, which reveal that over time there is no substantive discount to shareholders for investing this way. In fact, if there is a variance, it has been shown to be a slight premium, if anything. Our friends who have developed the strategies in the SRI world have more years of data to show that people who have invested using those screens have, in fact, often done better. You can even compare an index they have developed known as the Domini Index to the other popular indexes and download performance over various periods, to convince yourself.

That leads to the next important issue for the BRI industry: You would do well to observe the work that the SRI industry has done to develop indexes, Exchange Traded Funds (ETFs) and other ways to draw investors to their concepts.

The fledgling nature of BRI as a startup industry is part of the problem. The providers of BRI have a responsibility to take this from a concept that currently appeals to a few believers and investors to the next level of credibility and understanding. The credibility part will require the current and future providers of BRI services to unite in an industry effort to speak with a common voice and to educate the investing public as to what the services mean and how they can be utilized. It also would serve to help other institutions observe and replicate their own versions of screening techniques that would bring more investment alternatives to the marketplace. This may sound like giving away the "keys to the kingdom" from a business standpoint, but, in fact, until this industry reaches critical mass with eight to ten providers of BRI services, many financial advisors will be reluctant to place all of their clients' funds in this investment mode.

WHEN WILL WE HAVE A BRI INDEX?

Another important step in gaining credibility in the marketplace is to develop a BRI index that reflects the common screenings of many of the BRI providers. It is not fair to investors to compare performance only to the secular indexes that contain many of the companies that believers do not wish to own. Comparing a portfolio that has been screened for BRI concerns with the DJIA 30 Industrials could have a low correlation because many of those companies are actually screened out. In the S&P 500 index, the correlation is higher, but, in fact, 15 to 18 percent of those issues are screened out. In the Russell 3000 Index, 10 to 15 percent are screened out. It will cost something to do this, and investors should expect that they may be paying some of this cost in the fees and expenses that some providers will charge. In general, most BRI providers have fees that are in line with their secular counterparts, and you will not notice a significant difference.

Why do all this? The fact is, BRI providers *are* competing in the secular marketplace, and while there is a need to show investors that there may be a cost to being a BRI investor. My belief is that investors who invest this way will profit both short and long term, but it is really about being honest with all concerned to show credible comparisons. Investors can obtain a lot of historical performance data from all types of sources on the Internet or through their advisors to investigate BRI providers.

Call to Action!

BRI Investors:

1. Start investigating all the providers listed in Chapter 6 and elsewhere to see if you are interested in investing with them.
2. Ask your financial advisor to help you seek BRI providers.
3. Find out from your pastor or friends if they are using any type of BRI applications and how they feel about the process.
4. Check out all sources you can find on the Internet on BRI services.

BRI Providers:

1. Unite in setting up a BRI forum and central planning entity for professional advancement.
2. Build a marketing program that will help investors understand BRI principles.
3. Develop a BRI index so that investors will have a legitimate benchmark.
4. Hire a full-time director of a BRI foundation to co-ordinate all of the above.

Mark Henry indicated that his greatest desire in this arena would be to have someone come along to put what he referred to as the "stamp of approval" for investors to know that an institution is committed to BRI. Naturally, this cannot be done, literally, as each provider is going to earn the right to work for investors based upon performance and service, but the idea is right on the money when it comes to bringing this idea to investors from the aspect of exposure.

If, for example, the mutual funds and money managers indicate in their literature that they subscribe to the principles of "BRI Marketing Arm for the Masses" or some similarly named organization, that might motivate an investor to move to the next level. As the big-picture provider of the vision for BRI, this professional entity would bring information and dialogue to the public, thus providing a good start toward total credibility and awareness with all the participants in the marketplace. Obviously, there are some dangers to this, as the standards need to be agreed upon by participants in the industry, and differences will need to be negotiated. But I strongly believe that it is time to move on to the next rung on the ladder of acceptance and credibility.

It should be noted that the S&P 500 Index (copyright Standard and Poor's Corporation) is the most often used index as a benchmark. This may or may not be appropriate, and, as we mentioned earlier in this chapter, the sooner the BRI industry develops a useful and appropriate index for BRI funds, the sooner all of the industry can increase its acceptance and credibility. Even with that having been said, the data provided shows that performance of these funds in recent years as they have gained critical mass has been very competitive with their secular competitors. If you are a believer and wish to split hairs about performance data while holding investments that sell pornography and profit from abortion, tobacco, alcohol or smut peddling, then I can only pray that you would come to your senses.

In a recent period, one of The Timothy Plan funds was ranked as the number one fund in its peer group by a study done for 2007. Even though this is just one short period of time, it is an indictor that many of the BRI funds and money managers are reaching a greater segment of the market in both volume and credibility. In the bear market debacle of 2008, many of these BRI providers suffered significant losses in their equity funds while performing above their benchmarks with their bond, and fixed income funds. Most of them recovered significantly in the recovery year of 2009. This is not to say that anyone should choose a BRI provider based on performance that will allow one to make more money because of ecclesiastical vision.

Performance statistics is one of the most abused and slanted areas of the financial services industry. The most strongly stated case I can give you from my experience on Wall Street is that BRI providers as a whole, will, over time, perform in a similar fashion to their secular competitors. If this is not enough to put you at ease about performance, then you are free to keep chasing rainbows and looking for the pot of gold. If anything, watch out for the incredible "out performers" as they may be overstating their numbers or even worse be padding their numbers similar to other "Ponzi" schemers. At the very least, they are probably guilty of using the wrong benchmark to overstate their performance which I would call a sin of commission!

PRAYER

Heavenly Father, I now recognize that I have not invested with your wishes in mind! As I consider all of the wealth you have allowed me to accumulate and manage on your behalf, I ask for your guidance and wisdom in investing in a way that would be pleasing to you. Forgive me for not understanding this relationship and for not being more aware of how "Your" funds are being used. Give me wisdom in seeking the best investments that also work to please you. Amen.

QUESTIONS TO CONSIDER

1. What about this concept of BRI and investing with Christ-like ideals? How would you describe the costs? How do you anticipate they will compare to an index fund?

2. What is the meaning of terms like benchmark and time-weighted rates of return?

3. Will you care enough to stick with a BRI strategy if investing this way proves to cost you money?

4. Where can someone find performance information? Why does it seem so hard to find?

8

How Do I Make a Difference (or Start a Movement)?

In my most evil moments I was convinced that I was doing good. And it was only when I lay there on rotting prison straw that I sensed within myself the first stirrings of good. Gradually it was disclosed to me that the line separating good and evil passes not through states nor through political parties but through every human heart. Alexander Solzhenitsyn

When someone finds out that I am a stock broker or, as we prefer to call ourselves today, a financial consultant or financial advisor, it is almost automatic that he or she shares a story about his or her own investing experiences. This usually includes their greatest stock tip or the exploits of one of their relatives who have made a bundle on this or that. I usually ask how that person is doing with that huge windfall and how he or she handled the tax bite that the gains brought with it. That's when the deer in the headlight look appears, and I often conclude that the gain was smaller than the original boast. In fact, the gains often turn out to be "paper gains." Paper gains are where people trade on paper without really risking their hard earned money. This may be fun, but it is not investing until the investor has placed money into the actual stock of a company.

So it is with BRI and the hoped for *Kingdom Gains* that will result from investors who wish to make a difference. Unless believers start to demand a different approach from their advisors, and, correspondingly, the advisors demand a different approach from their employers, life will stay pretty much the same.

WHERE DO WE GO FROM HERE?

BRI providers must continue to grow and provide a more unified approach to the market. This would include establishing a BRI benchmark as well as hard evidence of performance-related issues.

There is a dance around this issue because it is true that this industry is so young that there has been a shortage of established providers of BRI to fill the needs of investors. In order to attain proper diversification and representation across many asset classes, there are just not yet as many choices among BRI providers. Frankly, most of this negative talk is bound up in the fact that people don't like to change what they are doing—and greed starts to set in with the fear that a change might see their performance drop off. Couple that with advisors who don't really want to change what they are doing because it may cost them some credibility with clients for not having been more attuned to their clients' wishes—and the dance gets a partner.

Just as people who only trade on paper will only attain paper gains, investors who keep investing in companies whose practices result in sinful activities will never see or experience *Kingdom Gains*.

If you are a mutual fund investor, it is time to start searching for a mutual fund that invests like your heart and your Bible teaches you. Read the prospectus of the funds before you invest and decide if this way of investing sounds pleasing to God and to you. Keep looking and searching to find the fund or funds that you are comfortable with, in outlook. Always look at the top five or ten holdings in a fund; they also will give you a clue as to the type of companies in which the firm is placing its strongest weightings.

CAN SRI AND BRI CO-EXIST IN THE SAME INDUSTRY?

As the new kid on the block, BRI advocates have brought a new emphasis to an industry that was already loosely defined by many participants with varying concerns. There are even SRI participants whose screenings are similar to some of the BRI providers. As the dialogue continues to evolve, there will be many attempts to define segments of the industry so that investors will be clear on what choices are available. It may actually result in your finding funds which invest under more traditional SRI principles to fulfill what you wish with your investments. Even some of the old-school funds, such as the Pioneer Funds, Pax Funds and Franklin Templeton Funds, have screening techniques that represent investment management doing some moral screening, which could be a step in the right direction for you. While this may be considered a baby step, it's a good start if it leads you to where you need to go. Many funds have changed from their original purpose, and a close examination of the prospectus and the funds' holdings will give you clues as to whether these funds are for you.

The issue that is even more critical to approach is the unity of the BRI providers themselves, who must come together despite their differences to help investors recognize the efforts each provider is making.

A BRI CLEARING HOUSE?

I have met several men and women who could serve as the head of such an institution if the participants realized how important it is to come together as an industry. Having a spokesman who touches on current topics in the news and appears on the business channels during market hours, will not only lend credibility to the BRI efforts, but it will help to launch the benchmarks that will bring more credibility to the performance of the participants. Add to that the importance of educating the investing world about how BRI differs from secular investing, and this would provide additional growth for all involved. This also would be a natural way to relate back to the SRI world as it, too, will have many common ties to the screening and efforts being made by BRI providers.

VOTE THE PROXY!

If you invest on your own in individual stocks and bonds, find out as much as you can about the companies before buying or retaining them. Ask your advisor about how to best screen for companies that you, as a Christian, wish to avoid. Once you have built a portfolio, there are some benefits from direct ownership in stocks. In addition to receiving the annual reports directly from the companies you own, you also will receive a proxy to vote as you wish, regarding corporate matters. All of these are available online, as well as through snail mail.

When the proxy comes each year, vote it! Don't throw it away! When you see most proxies, you will find they are very minimal on information and very strong on advocating how to vote. It is often true that agreeing with management helps the shareholders. One of the areas that this is rarely the case, however, is in the area of stock and incentive options. Those options are always advantageous for management and employees, and many times cause dilution in the current holdings of the shareholders. Notice that in 2007 the rules finally required some sort of explanation of cost, but the cost figures still are not posted on the proxy itself but buried in pages of figures and charts. This is often a flagrant violation of shareholder trust, as many stock option plans have rewarded upper management and officers for the most mediocre and even negative performances to shareholders. There was a study done in 2008 and 2009 that indicated that excessive compensation for top executives actually brought about worse results for the shareholders, not better.

How Should I Vote?

What to do? Vote against or abstain from all directors, starting immediately, unless they become more open about the cost of stock options and stock incentives on the proxy card itself? Right now the law says they must provide something in a supplement, but the average shareholder is entitled to more than that. If they wish to gain your vote approving millions or billions in stock options, the least they can do is estimate how much that will cost. Going one step further, how about comparing the cost of the stock options to the average of the last three years' earnings of the company? That would compare, side by side, what the shareholders' earnings are, to a handful of executives who are often the recipients of these inflated compensation packages. Providing a simple calculation known as dilution or maximum dilution based on the maximum exercise of all stock options, could be included on the proxy, itself. Until management starts to provide that, I vote against all option plans that do NOT tell me, as a shareholder, how much it will cost me. This seems like such an easy change for the SEC to mandate, but so far no progress has been made to help shareholders with transparency.

Figure 8-1 offers a sample proxy from the 2006 annual meeting of Seagate Technologies. I am not advocating this company as a buy or a sell, nor are we suggesting that this proxy is a good or bad format, as most proxies look just like this one. It is my intent to use this proxy as a way to illustrate how various issues are presented to shareholders.

Notice how the company breaks out issue 1A thru 1L to list all the directors, individually, for voting, which is quite progressive; most companies just offer a slate of candidates for the shareholders approval. Notice, however, issues 2 and 3 are their requests for shareholder approval for issuing 36 million shares under issue 2, and 10 million shares under issue 3. Investors could study the plans in more detail to see how these shares would be distributed and over what time periods, but there is still no indication of how much this request is going to cost shareholders. As it turns out, the request under issue 2 represents a request for about $830 million and a dilution of about 2 to 3 percent of the existing shareholders equity. Plan 3 seems less costly because employees are purchasing these shares, even though it is likely at a discount to the market. I am not offering an opinion as to whether the plans are good or bad, but rather the information being supplied to shareholders is adequate to make an intelligent decision. This company has been quite cyclical in its earnings history so by studying its last three years of earning, we see two years where earnings were much higher than the $830 million, and one year that was a loss. These options will, in all likelihood, be distributed to employees over a period of years and also exercised over more years so the entire cost of the $830 million is not known for sure. Notice that the directors recommend a vote in favor of all these issues.

SEAGATE TECHNOLOGY ANNUAL MEETING TO BE HELD ON 10/26/06
FOR HOLDERS AS OF 09/01/06

51119   77-1362   YOU MAY ENTER YOUR VOTING INSTRUCTIONS AT 1-800-474-
OR WWW.PROXYVOTE.COM UP UNTIL 11:59 PM EASTERN TIME THE
DAY BEFORE THE CUT-OFF OR MEETING DATE.

DIRECTORS

PROPOSAL(S)	DIRECTORS RECOMMEND
1A - ELECT AS A DIRECTOR. ----------------->>>	FOR --->>>
1B - ELECT AS A DIRECTOR. ----------------->>>	FOR --->>>
1C - ELECT AS A DIRECTOR. ----------------->>>	FOR --->>>
1D - ELECT AS A DIRECTOR. ----------------->>>	FOR --->>>
1E - ELECT AS A DIRECTOR. ----------------->>>	FOR --->>>
1F - ELECT AS A DIRECTOR. ----------------->>>	FOR --->>>
1G - ELECT AS A DIRECTOR. ----------------->>>	FOR --->>>
1H - ELECT AS A DIRECTOR. ----------------->>>	FOR --->>>
1I - ELECT AS A DIRECTOR. ----------------->>>	FOR --->>>
1J - ELECT AS A DIRECTOR. ----------------->>>	FOR --->>>
1K - ELECT AS A DIRECTOR. ----------------->>>	FOR --->>>
1L - ELECT AS A DIRECTOR. ----------------->>>	FOR --->>>
➡ 2 - APPROVE AN INCREASE IN SHARES ELIGIBLE FOR ISSUANCE UNDER 2004 --->>> STOCK COMPENSATION PLAN IN THE AMOUNT OF 36 MILLION SHARES.	FOR --->>>
➡ 3 - APPROVE AN INCREASE IN THE ISSUABLE SHARES FOR PURCHASE UNDER --->>> EMPLOYEE STOCK PURCHASE PLAN IN THE AMOUNT OF 10 MILLION SHARES.	FOR --->>>
4 - RATIFY THE APPOINTMENT OF ERNST & YOUNG LLP TO SERVE AS ---------->>> INDEPENDENT REGISTERED ACCOUNTING FIRM.	FOR --->>>

Figure 8-1 Example Proxy Statement from Seagate Technology

If more than 50 percent of the shareholders of this company had voted against these measures, the company would have had to come up with a different approach and perhaps a different plan. Christians, as a group of shareholders, could easily have made up 50 percent of this company's shareholders so the potential for influence is tremendous. This same veto power in the wrong hands also could be a tragedy, if used in the wrong way. With the abuse of power and excessive compensation plans that are going on in companies today, it is a risk worth taking. So many of the performance-related bonuses and stock awards are little more than a small group of executives figuring out a way to lay off thousands of workers to save money short term on salaries and benefits. They then take credit for the bump in earnings and reward themselves with the savings from the pockets of the laid-off workers. This is not productivity, and many of those same people being laid off could make the company more profitable long term, if given a chance. In essence, the top managements of many companies have used their shareholders and the company's assets as a sort of personal ATM machine via the stock options and benefits that we have unwittingly approved, by just going along with them.

DILUTION

The one concept that could change this entire problem of visibility is simply to report on the maximum possible dilution that any of these programs will cost the shareholder. This is a simple calculation and could be carried on every proxy form for every request to tap into the "ATM Machine" of shareholders' money. Notice that there is no reference to dilution on the proxy.

Proxy cards also have a place to write your own concerns and plaudits for the company. If you as a shareholder observe the positive things those companies are doing, write them about that as well, because that reinforces positive behavior.

WARNING! UNSCRUPULOUS PEOPLE COULD USE BRI FOR THEIR OWN GAIN

Given the history of many movements that get started with good intentions, Christians have often seen how good intentions can turn into bad results. For example, when many jumped on the bandwagon about the pitfalls of our society moving into the

132

21st century, we had many snake oil salesmen spouting Scripture and inciting a Y2K panic. Likewise, many of our country's financial hardships are compounded by some taking advantage of the poor. Debt, including the government's deficits, is cited as cause and effect for more maladies than I can imagine. Because almost everyone has a mortgage or some debt on credit cards, whole industries have been developed to deal with that guilt trip. Our best hope for success in the BRI movement is that believers start to take stewardship seriously, not only in their portfolios, but also as it relates to their relationship with God. As you place all of you and your assets on the altar for God's glory, remember you have been blessed with a brain to reason and think through issues for yourself.

There are serious people who wonder if the term BRI shouldn't be changed to MRI for Morally Responsible Investing. The concern is that to use the Bible in the same sense as a style of investing is to capture a false impression of one person being right and all others being wrong, if we don't agree. Yet the Bible is clear about what will happen to those who would abuse God's Word(s) for personal gain and possibly inflict harm on others (Jeremiah 23:28-32). Even after considering all of this, it seems that Christians must find ways to show the world, through their example, that we are different and that we are salt and light even in the world of investing!

DRAW YOUR LINE IN THE SAND SOMEWHERE!

Is this issue serious enough for you to change what you are doing? Can you face yourself in the mirror by saying that how you are invested and deriving returns on your funds makes you a likely candidate to hear, "Well done my good and faithful servant?" As you ponder what the Lord would call you to do, the sagest advice is:, "Draw a line in the sand somewhere!" A checklist of possible actions is offered as a starting point to determine where you will draw that line:

1. Check all your holdings, one-by-one to consider if they still belong on your side of the line.
2. Pray about what your investment philosophy and strategy should be, going forward. Does it include helping others as well as yourself? This should, of course, include your spouse.
3. Write down specific goals after completing #2 and share them with your current advisor(s).
4. Listen carefully to how your advisor is approaching any plans to help you achieve any changes in your objectives.
5. Decide if the suggestions for change will give you a greater sense that your wishes will be implemented.
6. Determine that if your assets are being held by a retirement plan that the custodian of the plan can help you find investments that are acceptable.
7. Review your estate plan to see if family members would be properly cared for, but not necessarily spoiled.
8. Review your estate plan to see if you are including God's work in how you are leaving assets behind.
9. Pray and share together the plans you have and the ideals that you wish to incorporate into your investments, with a trusted friend. Without sharing numbers or bragging rights, see what their thoughts are about your efforts.

- Place a date on your calendar to review this list every year.

THE 5-PERCENT RULE APPLIED TO LIVING

The rest of my action plan for investors and especially for those who are working on their retirement plan, is to adopt the 5-percent rule. This has been a popular plan for endowment funds and institutional investors when trying to determine how much of their capital they can consume in any one year and still be all right 25 or 50 years from now. It works like this: If you have $1 million as a nest egg or $100,000, and you want to know how much of that you can spend, the 5-percent rule says you can safely spend $50,000 or $5,000 this year. If next year it is worth $1.1 million, then you can spend $55,000 that year. If it is worth $900,000, you can spend $45,000. Once your lifestyle is in tune with this pattern, you will be able to respect the blessings of wealth and also become more generous, both now and in your estate planning.

Furthermore, consider the responsibility involved if you were to leave $200,000 from your estate to a church or ministry. Instead, consider leaving some or all of it in the form of an endowment similar to this, so that the recipient is not spoiled by the windfall. The only time you allow yourself to violate the 5-percent rule is for true emergencies and to give it away for the Lord's work. **Once you become committed to this concept, you will find that you don't need to raise your living standard every time your wealth increases, and you will be able to give more.**

Critics of this plan often indicate that endowments can spoil a church or make others rely on the endowments rather than continue the outreach and work that made the church vital and healthy in the first place. I would contend that churches don't die from the money they receive; they die from losing their first love of sharing the gospel and being a light to the world. They die because the passion they once had, has changed to going through the motions.

Other critics argue that this seems akin to storing up your possessions on earth rather than sending them ahead. Both could be right! But too many people are so certain that the Lord is coming soon and thus aren't making the slightest financial plans. My question is, "What if He tarries another 2,000 years before He returns?"

We might be wasting billions and trillions on the McMansions and Mercedes while that same wealth could be structured and set aside for ministry to the poor and for those who do not know

Christ. So find the investments that will be pleasing to God, be a witness in your dealings with your advisors, vote your proxies to the glory of God, remember to care for your family first, as that is what God expects of you, and be creative in seeking the Lord's will in how you will leave a legacy with the blessings of wealth you have received. Spoiling your children or your favorite charity by giving too much too fast is not good stewardship.

QUESTIONS TO CONSIDER

1. Are you ready to make a difference? Are you thinking of just you and your family, or also of those in your sphere of influence?

2. What steps do you wish to take to start doing things differently?

3. What is a proxy and why should anyone have to concern themselves with that?

4. If you are retired, how are you determining your income budget from your nest egg? If you are still working, how do you budget for now and balance your saving needs for the future?

9

WHAT DOES THE BIBLE REALLY TEACH?

*I had built my prosperity theology on a few isolated, misinter-
preted verses of Scripture...As I pored over the Word of God, the
Holy Spirit used the Scriptures to convince me that I, like so
many of my former colleagues, had merely been preaching what
I had heard other preachers say. I passed along things I had
read in somebody else's books, rather than carefully examining
the Scriptures to see what God had to say. I was an unwitting
false prophet.* Jim Bakker

The premise for this overview of biblical references is built
around the teachings of Paul in Romans 14. God reveals his truth
in unique ways for each believer, and on a timetable that is consistent with our walk and growth. It is important for each man to be

convinced in his own mind and heart that these issues are valid for adoption. To put this chapter in context, it is very important before you read on, that you pause and again read Romans 14 from the Bible.

Romans 14:5 says, "One man considers one day more sacred than another; another man considers every day alike. Each one should be fully convinced in their own mind." As you seek God's will for your investments, allow the words of the Bible to guide you in this effort.

When Jesus walked this earth, there was no New York Stock Exchange or democracies which fostered capitalism. There were, however, many examples of riches and wealth that easily transcend time, to offer insight into what Jesus taught about money and its attributes. It is intended that readers investigate the Scripture passages listed below, and develop their own thoughts about how the Bible teaches us to act upon this issue. Just as Solomon chose wisdom as the greatest gift God could endow upon him, you too will become wiser and will benefit by reading the Word to become a better investor.

Wisdom
Proverbs 3:9-11
Proverbs 8:11
Proverbs 16:16
James 1:5

Riches
Proverbs 11:28
Mark 10:23-25

Parables
Matthew 13:44-46
Matthew 25:14-30

Luke 7:41-43
Luke 12:16-21
Luke 18:9-14

Many Christian Financial Professionals have adopted their own biblical rationale for BRI concerns. Richard Sadowski is one such member of Kingdom Advisors, and his clients receive the following information when considering an association with his firm:

WHY CONSIDER BIBLICALLY RESPONSIBLE INVESTMENT SELECTION?

Most investors are unaware that their investments may be supporting the very things they are morally opposed to. Investing money, irrespective of your values, will fund a future that may be void of your values. For these reasons, prayerfully consider the following biblical principles when making your investment decisions. *"Do not be conformed to this world, but be transformed by the renewing of your mind, that by testing you may discern what is the will of God."* Rom 12:2.

1. IT'S NOT OUR MONEY

The earth is the LORD's and the fullness thereof, the world and those who dwell therein. Psalm 24:1

Beware lest you say in your heart, "My power and the might of my hand have gotten me this wealth." You shall remember the LORD your God, for it is he who gives you power to get wealth. Deuteronomy 8:17-18

2. AS CHRISTIANS, OUR LIFE BELONGS TO GOD

You are not your own, for you were bought with a price. 1 Corinthians 6:19-20.

It is no longer I who live, but Christ who lives in me. Galatians 2:20.

3. WE ARE STEWARDS (CARETAKERS) OF GOD'S WEALTH

This is how one should regard us, as servants of Christ and stewards of the mysteries of God. 1 Corinthians 4:1

For it will be like a man going on a journey, who called his servants and entrusted to them his property. Matthew 25:14

4. WE WILL BE HELD ACCOUNTABLE

It is required of stewards that they be found trustworthy. 1 Corinthians 4:2

So then each of us will give an account of himself to God. Romans 14:12

We at Christian Financial Principles believe that God will also hold us accountable for how we advise you to manage His assets. We take our responsibility to you and to God very seriously. Biblically Responsible Investment Selection is a difficult and ongoing process, but we are committed to offering you this service and encourage you to, as much as possible, avoid those investments that violate biblical principles. *"Try to discern what is pleasing to the Lord. Take no part in the unfruitful works of darkness, but instead expose them."* Ephesians 5:10-11

Rob Cathcart, executive director of IHS Foundation in Northeast Ohio, has developed a biblical rationale for endowment, which is another aspect of investing that involves a combination of both investing for now and considering an estate plan that has a longer term giving strategy. The following is that foundation's guidelines for how biblical truth encourages this:

Is Endowment biblical? Sooner or later, any Christian ministry that wants to start or build an endowment must wrestle with this question. Most Christians are familiar with the Bible's teaching on giving back to God as He provides for us—more commonly understood as tithing from income. Yet many Christians and ministries are in uncharted territory as they begin to think about the subject of endowment building from a biblical perspective.

- The word "endowment" does not appear in the Bible. Like many other modern concepts (evolution or abortion, for example) we must search the Scriptures and apply principles that are consistent, unambiguous and relevant to the topic to begin to feel like we are standing on solid biblical ground. The following are presented in this light for what they teach about endowment:
- In Genesis, God declares, "Behold I have given you every plant yielding seed that is on the surface of all the earth, and every tree which has fruit yielding seed; it shall be food for you;" (1:29) and later to Noah and his family, "every moving thing that is alive shall be food for you; I give all to you, as I gave the green plant" (9:3) From these we learn that God provided food for people; a renewable resource in its season. This endowment of life is a perpetual provision for the needs of humanity.
- Later in Genesis, Joseph, inspired by God, tells Pharaoh to "exact a fifth of the produce of the land of Egypt in the seven years of abundance. Then let them gather all the food of these good years that are coming, and store up the grain for food in the cities under Pharaoh's authority, and let them

guard it. And let the food become as a reserve for the land for the seven years of famine which will occur in the land of Egypt." (41:34-36) This principal of saving from the good years to provide for the coming years of famine saved not only the Egyptians, but also Joseph's entire family. Later, God made a provision for His people and their future from the wealth of Egypt as they departed (Exodus 12:35, 36). The provision was necessary for them to have as they wandered and settled in their new land.

- In Leviticus we learn of the principle of the Sabbath Year in farming and the Year of Jubilee. God promised to "...so order my blessing for you in the sixth year that it will bring forth the crop for three years. When you are sowing the eighth year, you can still eat old things from the crop, eating the old until the ninth year when its crop comes in." (25:21, 22) This extra provision of God's was to provide for the future needs of the people (also Exodus 16:5).

- King David's heart desire was to build a Temple to God in Jerusalem. In 1 Chronicles we learn how "*David prepared large quantities of iron to make the nails for the doors of the gates and for the clamps, and more bronze than could be weighed; and timers of cedar logs beyond number.*" (22:3,4) and how he with great pains "*prepared for the house of the Lord 100,000 talents of gold and 1,000,000 talents of silver, and bronze, and iron beyond weight, for they are in great quantity; also timber and stone I have prepared.*" (v. 14) David provided in one generation for the spiritual work of the next generation.

What was God's opinion of David's desire to endow the building of the Temple? In 1 Chronicles we read of the establishment of God's Covenant with David. God sends word to David the very night He first plans to do this, promising to establish David's throne forever. David is overcome by

God's promise and blessing and recognizes how God "has promised this good thing to Thy servant. And now it hath pleased Thee to bless the house of Thy servant, that it may continue forever before Thee." (17:26, 27) Clearly God was pleased.

- In Matthew we read about how the wise men presented "gifts of gold and frankincense and myrrh." (2:11) These gifts were undoubtedly used by the Holy Family as a provision for food, shelter and clothing as they fled to Egypt as refugees for a few years.

- From these we teach the principal that God provides for specific purposes or needs that will arise in the future. Often His provision for those future needs is to meet them from a "bumper crop" today, taking from a current abundance and setting it aside for His specific purpose.

- Later in Matthew, Jesus instructs us: "Do not lay up for yourselves treasures upon earth, where moth and rust destroy, and where thieves break in and steal. But lay up for yourselves treasures in heaven, where neither moth nor rust destroys, and where thieves do not break in or steal." (6:19, 20) The laying up of treasures in heaven includes making provision from today's abundance to meet a spiritual need God has spoken about in the next generation, provided we do not neglect the needs of those around us today.

- Jesus also teaches in the Parable of the Talents, that we will give an account to the master upon his return. If we have a gain to show, from what He entrusted to us, He will say, "Well done, good and faithful servant; you were faithful with a few things, I will put you in charge of many things; enter into the joy of your master." (5:21) In other words, it pleases Him that we put into production and reap growth from what He entrusts to us, including our stewardship of giving.

- As a final point, we read in Acts 15 of the outcome, repeated three times, from the Council in Jerusalem. Resulting from a crisis within the early church as Gentiles began to come to faith in Jesus, the dispute centered on what should be required of them regarding the Law of Moses.
- *"Then it seemed good to the apostles and the elders, with the whole church..." (v. 22),*

  "It seemed good to us, having become of one mind..." (v.25),

  "For it seemed good to the Holy Spirit and to us..." (v. 28)

  Here we see the principle of church leadership (elders) reacting to changing circumstances around them and making prayerful and well-thought-through decisions regarding the Lord's work. If done by qualified leadership in a humble attitude of serving others, Christians are to accept the outcome. For example, argumentative Paul does not question the council's decision, nor do the legalistic Jewish Christians. This is accomplished under the authority Christ, Himself, gave the church.

  From all of the above, we may distill several key issues regarding endowment:
- Does the ministry or need to be endowed have a biblical mandate?
- Will an individual steward of God's resources—a person—be taking a God-pleasing step of stewardship by participating in giving?
- Will the establishment of an endowment harm or compliment the faith-giving of the stewards who regularly support this work now?

- Have proper safeguards been established so that God's property will not be "storehoused" (i.e. hoarded) but instead be a flowing source of meeting real and ongoing spiritual or physical need?
- Do the leaders of the church or ministry, after prayer and seeking God, believe, in unity, that they are doing the right thing in establishing an endowment for future spiritual work?

†

God entrusts wealth to individuals. Many Americans have recently experienced "bumper crop years" and desire to provide for God's work in the future from their abundance. Scripture clearly gives many examples where this is legitimate, and even further, pleasing to God. As a result, ministries who possess an endowable mission should offer this stewardship opportunity to their supporters.

Nancy Currid of Stewardship Advisors and the Biblically Responsible Investing Institute (BRII) has done considerable research on both the basis for BRI and the practical application of those principles in screening companies for investment. The following is an excerpt from her document, "The Scriptural Basis for Biblically Responsible Investing" published in June 2006. The complete report can be viewed on the BRII website.

> The Parable of the Talents (Matthew 25:14-30) reminds Christians that they are to be industrious and faithful with their Master's resources. Indeed, to whom much has been given, much will be demanded (Luke 12:47-49). Yet several biblical principles, in particular, restrain Christians from falling to the world's mindset that profit and rate of return are all that matter.

For one thing, there is the first commandment (Exodus 20:3). God requires His people to worship, honor and glorify Him alone. They are to have no other god, including the god of materialism, net worth and rate of return.

Second, human life is sacred. Man, as God's image bearer, is precious and inherently valuable. Consequently, all purposeful business activity should benefit mankind. Likewise, businesses should exhibit justice, mercy and compassion. Man should not be destroyed, injured, corrupted, exploited, preyed upon or dehumanized simply for the sake of profit.

The principles of justice, mercy and compassion are especially noteworthy given their prevalence in Old Testament law. God built into Hebrew society a concern for the most vulnerable members of society. The Sabbatical system (Leviticus 25, Deuteronomy 15) provided regular rest as well as protection from life-long enslavement, indebtedness and the loss of one's inheritance. Gleaning laws provided food for the poor, the alien and the widows (Leviticus 19:9-10). The Kinsman Redeemer (Ruth 2-4) was a means of rescue for an enslaved, indebted or disinherited relative. Other laws stipulate compassionate treatment of the poor worker (Deuteronomy 24:10-15). Needless to say, mercy and compassion are of paramount interest to God.

Holiness should further influence and guide the Christian investor. God declares that He is holy; therefore He demands His people to be holy (Leviticus 11:44-45; 19:2; 20:26; cf. 1 Peter 1:15-

16). Inherent in the word holiness is the idea of being set apart. God is set apart in the sense of being majestically exalted above all He created and in terms of being pure, perfect, separated from sin (Exodus 3, Isaiah 6). Therefore, when God calls His people to be holy, He is commanding separation from sin and conformity to His image. He is instructing His people, individually and corporately, to be distinctive, righteous, wholly consecrated to Him.

Finally, Christian investors must be mindful of the charge to be salt and light (Matthew 5:13-16). Believers are to be exemplary in their behavior, above reproach, without guile (Psalm 32:2; 1 Peter 2:1). By their upright actions, Christians are to silence unbelieving critics (1 Peter 2:15; cf. Proverbs 16:7) and bear witness to their Savior. Thus there is a genuine testimonial aspect in one's investing.

Biblically Responsible Investing, then, for the Christian incorporates a desire to serve Christ alone, not mammon. It embraces the sanctity and dignity of mankind, principles of justice, mercy and compassion. Furthermore, it includes a commitment to holiness, for the honor of God and the salvation of unbelievers.

†

As you can see, there is no lack of opinions about how God cares about all of our activities, including our investments. It is more than obvious to me that trying to please God with this aspect of our stewardship is going to take on more importance as believers balance the call of the Scriptures with the reality of saving and investing.

QUESTIONS TO CONSIDER

1. This information is covered in more detail in the *Kingdom Gains* Study Guide available on the website. Have you purchased your copy?

2. What does Romans 13 and 14 say about issues such as BRI for each believer?

3. It has been recorded that the Bible refers to wealth and money in more than 2,500 different verses. What story or passage speaks to you about how to handle money and wealth?

4. What lessons do you find most poignant about the story of the rich man who questions Jesus about what he must do to find eternal life? (Matthew 19:16-22; Mark 10:13-16 and Luke 18:18-24). Do you think that means all of us should sell what we have and give it to the poor? Does it mean that we should all follow him?

10

BUY, SELL, HOLD OR PRAY

Ordinary riches can be stolen; real riches cannot. In your soul are
infinitely precious things that cannot be taken from you.
Oscar Wilde

What do you do when the financial world is in turmoil and you
are in the midst of the storm?

Recent periods of distress in the financial markets have caused
many to stop in their tracks and ask hard questions about themselves and their future. Government bailouts and bankruptcy
threats abounded during 2007 to 2008, and advisors and investors felt like they were in the eye of a hurricane with names like
Paulson, Cox and Bernanke making headlines. Even the election
of President Barak Obama was in great part due to the financial
woes of the time.

149

By this point in the book you know that I spent more than 34 years as a financial advisor at Merrill Lynch (1971-2005), and my response to the events of that period was shock and frustration. One of the trademark traits of a Merrill Lynch advisor was to never be surprised at any event that happens in the marketplace, as it should be both predictable and logical. That period was neither of those for me!

The reasoning behind our lack of fear was because we all felt we worked for the biggest, smartest, most informed firm. Most advisors have used this concept in their approach to clients, and it takes many forms at every firm. At Merrill Lynch, we always thought we had the most analysts, the most advisors or, in many cases, we had the most capital. In reflecting on past years, many of the long-time employees had a sense that the company was moving quickly away from our traditional business philosophy. As this initially showed great earnings and results, the hubris kept growing, that this was good.

WAKE UP AND SMELL THE COMING STORM

If this was a wakeup call for me and others who work at the large Wall Street firms, then it should be a similar experience for others. No matter how much money your company has and no matter how much money you have, that is no match for the events of this life if God wants to place you in the crucible. If you are cruising along, and life is wonderful, that's great—but beware! Sooner or later you may find yourself and your family suffering financial stress.

Many friends and fellow advisors at Merrill would discuss how much leverage was actually going on beneath the surface of our company, and we feared that our management may be borrowing as much as 10 to 12 times our net worth.

When it was revealed to be more like 30 times our net worth, that rattled even a grizzled veteran like me. This was misplaced confidence in the world's version of strength. In the aftermath of that time, only the efforts of government officials and the acquisition by Bank of America saved the old Merrill Lynch from bankruptcy.

This was my own version of placing my faith and trust in the wrong things. Big powerful Wall Street firms and financial prowess with visible signs of wealth, permeate our society and create the myth of happiness through wealth. If you find yourself measuring your value and security by the size of your net worth or the position of power you might occupy, you are setting yourself up for great disappointment, as all of these things will perish. Recognizing your own value system is the best place to start the analysis of how to survive during such periods. Reverting back to the truths from earlier chapters about realizing that God owns it all, gives us a great starting point to get the rest right.

No doubt that during my time at Merrill, I was aware of the importance of the witness God was calling me to share. But I also got caught up in much of the same hubris of my company. The company would have been better off if it had followed the advice we gave to our clients, which was to stay out of debt unless there was a firm plan for repayment. Knowing that our clients' interests always came first, this concept was lost by our management as well as our competitors. The new standard became the goal of doing more transactions and collecting more fees, regardless of the economics of those transactions.

During previous years of market turmoil (1920 to 1935) there was a man named Daniel Drew who coined the phrase about short sellers: "He who sells what isn't his'n, buys it back or goes to prison." The new phrase for Wall Street at the start of the 21st century appeared to be, "He who borrows like water from a spout, pays it back or begs the Fed to bail them out."

BE SURE GOD EXPOSES GREED

So what lessons can believers learn from a financial crisis and turmoil such as this period in our history? When people cut corners and compromise their standards to make more money, those actions are followed by the eventual disclosure of those tactics. Write offs and losses from those actions were in the billions, and eventually the government had to spend trillions to bail us out!

Luke 12:1-3 RSV says, "In the meantime, when so many thousands of the multitudes had gathered together that they trod upon one another, he began to say to his disciples first, 'Beware of the leaven of the Pharisees, which is hypocrisy. Nothing is covered up that will not be revealed, or hidden that will not be known. Whatever you have said in the dark shall be heard in the light, and what you have whispered in private rooms shall be proclaimed upon the housetops.'"

PREPARE FOR THE INEVITABLE

As Christians trying to learn from these events, there are many ways to tackle this. The most compelling way of dealing with a crisis is to compare it to the second coming of Christ. We know He is coming, but we are commanded to work through our calling in such a way as to leave a witness. Yet all the references that we have about how to prepare for this wonderful day can still be frightening. Read these Bible passages for a chilling reminder of what's to come:

Luke 12:35-45 (a thief in the night); Matthew 20:1-16 (laborers in the vineyard);

Matthew 25:31-46 (separating sheep from goats); Luke 12:16-20 (rich fool);

Luke 16:19-31 (rich man and Lazarus).

So how do we balance the unexpected with something we are certain will happen? You can count on future times of financial chaos as well as times of great prosperity. The balance between the greed that is in the hearts of men and the seeds of capitalism and its ability to create worldly wealth are clearly a test from God to see if we will handle both extremes. The Bible does warn that rich people will have a hard time getting into heaven because their reliance on wealth often replaces reliance on Him. When this conflict hits, my answer is to repeat Matthew 6:33 from my mind and my heart. It's a good time to highlight your Bible if it is not already in bright colors!

TIPS FROM A TRUSTWORTHY SOURCE

Many books have been published both on how to get rich as well as how to handle financial meltdowns. In 2008, a book by Ronald Blue (see his comments in the Preface of this book) and Jeremy White, entitled *Surviving Financial Meltdown*, was clearly directed at Christians. Ron, who also is the president of Kingdom Advisors, made numerous public appearances to support the issues that are in the book. He talked time and again about the same five principles that will apply now and in the future for how to be a survivor and also to live out the biblical principles of this same concept:

1. Turn down the noise of the world and turn up God's voice! Stop watching CNBC as much, stop listening to the financial gurus and add time for your personal devotions.
2. Deal with reality. Take responsibility and face your fears.
3. Know where you are going. Check your spending and know your goals.
4. Have a plan. Reducing debt and increasing savings are often a good starting point.
5. Invest in eternity. Be generous even when it is hard.

If you expect that there will someday be another downturn in the economy and that you will need to be ready for it, these economic traumas will not be as personally disastrous.

Consider the story of the rich fool in Luke 12:13-21. He was so successful that he filled his barns to capacity. In fact, his crops were so abundant that he had grain and food stuffs greater than his storage capacity. His first thought was to take all of that bounty and build more barns and store it up for himself so he would never have to work again. Eat, drink and be merry, however, sounded like a better philosophy of life—one adopted as we have seen by many in our own country. But God called this man a "fool," and that night his life ended because he had decided to live that way.

This is similar to why our world goes through periods of scarcity and periods of excess. God knows we cannot handle excess for long periods of time or we will have the same philosophy of life as the rich fool. We will build more and bigger houses and join the "eat, drink and be merry" crowd unless we have those contrary reminders. Perhaps this is the very problem that has been fed by prophets of a prosperity gospel.

WHY ARE RICH PEOPLE OFTEN SO SAD AND LONELY?

Lonely people are usually unable to share their wealth or themselves with others. Generous people are not happier because they give to many people. Generous people are happier because they have found that giving creates an inward joy that cannot be duplicated in any other way. You may need to work on that very aspect in your life as well!

Notice the rich fool gave no hint that he was considering sharing this bounty with anyone else. In all of my years in advising clients on how to create wealth and then to use it wisely, **the people who cannot be generous are the closest thing to being dead, even if they are still living.** Finding that delicate balance of discerning how much is enough for you and your family is a worthy starting point to live in balance with God's will. To be a good witness as the steward of the blessings of worldly wealth is one of the tests that you and the Lord will reconcile someday. When in doubt, recite or reread Matthew 6:33: "But seek first his kingdom and his righteousness, and all these things will be given to you as well."

In short, stay away from margin accounts and keep your borrowing to modest levels. Some may even say be debt free, but it is not the debt itself that is the problem. It is excessive debt just as the love of money is the root of many evils.

QUESTIONS TO CONSIDER

1. When you think of going through a financial crisis, what's your state of mind?

2. In the past, when you faced difficult times, what helped you to find your way out?

3. Why does it seem like financial crises in our times are different from the ones of previous times?

4. Can you remember and apply the formula for handling a future crisis according to the principles offered by Ronald Blue?

5. Do you believe that biblical truth can help you when you are facing a grave financial matter? What evidence can you give to support that position?

11

Do You Relate?

What concerns me is my person, my salvation, my faith, my eternal life, etc. We always center the matter on ourselves. But Jesus did just the opposite...If I can let go of my preoccupation with self, my approach to the Bible changes immediately. I cannot continue to construct a theology of personal salvation. What matters is the other. I must not make use of the Bible for my own ends, but rather take myself out of the picture as much as possible.
Jacques Ellul

Most of my career at Merrill Lynch was consumed by my desire to serve my clients and to extend every effort to maximize the returns they could achieve. The concept of BRI was not at the forefront of my objectives when trying to help clients reach their goals early in my career. There never was a time, however, when I recommended a stock that brought products/services that were counter to my own set of values. Those values were couched in the biblical basis of my faith, and so, indirectly, I may have been starting to move toward a position that emulates what BRI providers are doing in an intentional way today.

My indoctrination to this idea of screening for BRI started when I was a member of the investment advisory committee for a regional division of the United Church of Christ known as the Western Reserve Association in Northeast Ohio. I was appointed to the board in the mid 1970s and served for more than 30 years, both as a participant and later on as an advisor on part of the funds. It was through my association with wonderful and committed members of that committee that we realized the struggle associated with investing funds that were entrusted to us and yet should reflect the type of holdings that were consistent with our faith.

We spent many sessions together talking about the Sullivan Principles and whether any company doing business of any kind in South Africa would qualify for retention in our portfolios. We all grew through those discussions, and I appreciated the people who respectfully disagreed with me. We always walked out of those rooms as brothers and sisters in the Lord when all the talking was done. We also gained respect for the process of trying to decide how to invest and be an extension of our testimony for Christ. I trust that you will do the same if you are relating to a body of people who govern the investment activities of which you are a part.

In 2005, it was my thrill to actually spend time in South Africa as part of a basketball team that competed in and around Cape Town. As we visited black, white and mixed-race schools to share the gospel and meet kids, I discovered a new appreciation for how far that country had come, but also saw how much potential was still untapped. The poverty and educational experiences that still miss the mark for so many kids remind me that we have so many places to go where we can provide help. It doesn't take long in Africa to think about the merits of BRI and even SRI when it comes to helping people. Can micro loans and strategic investing make a difference there? Probably yes, if there is someone who will help to administer and provide management for the investment of capital.

Even prior to my experience in Cape Town, I was privileged to go to Kenya with a basketball team that was able to see great things happen when our kids would share the gospel one-on-one with kids from the schools and with the kids we were competing against on the basketball courts of Mombasa. I will always remember my fellow leaders, Frank Stretar and Dave Piper, who also brought their sons, as well as kids from Cuyahoga Valley Christian Academy, and a very special young man from Berea, Greg Cooley. As we ministered according to Jeremiah 33:3, one great lesson that we learned about the power of prayer and humility affects me every day.

Our first few days in Kenya were good but not very effective in sharing our faith. We didn't think our messages were connecting with the kids, and although there were no truly negative incidents, we recognized that something was missing.

TIME TO GET DOWN ON MY KNEES

During our daily time together as a team, Frank shared with us that we needed to humble ourselves before God before He could work through us. As he got down on his knees to pray, one by one, we all followed him until we were all on our knees in prayer. The next day saw the start of more kids coming to know Christ than we could ever have expected.

Since that time in Kenya, I try to be on my knees for prayer at 11:45 p.m. every night. My wife has even made me move my prayer spot because she is upset at how I am wearing out the carpet in front of the chair in our great room! From that prayer time and through callings from other ministries, I have been blessed to visit and be part of mission projects in Morocco, Ukraine, Russia, El Salvador and France.

This African lesson in humility was important, but it is not how I would describe my entire career at Merrill Lynch. You may recall how my initial interview did not go so well, and it was a benevolent sales manager who sought me out to convince me to come to work there. The characters that were part of the office I entered, would be worth a lot of money if they could be featured in a television sitcom, but I suspect it could only be shown on pay-per-view cable. Back in 1971, the most successful people in that office were the ones who pretended to have inside information and would sell you the story of the day. Furthermore, they would lead you to believe that you were the only one receiving that golden nugget of information. If they convinced enough people of this, they would then enter orders and receive commissions based on this feeble line of rumors and half-truths. If it didn't work out, they would sell their people out a few days later and try another rumor, all the time collecting commissions on both buy and sell orders. This type of individual has been washed out of the industry for the most part and replaced by advisors who seek to find proper long-term solutions for their clients.

Luckily for me, there were several other brokers in that office who were of sound values and had great integrity. Those men and women were the ones who made me think it would be worth my time to keep making 90 to 100 calls per day to people I didn't know to try to encourage them to trust me with their money.

Eventually, the hard work did start to pay off. A few clients here and there, and all of a sudden you have some people who want to know your thoughts, take your advice and actually make money from what you suggest. This starts a power rush that gets bigger with every day that you work in the financial services business. Five years after I started, the market was still very bad, and clients were not making a lot of money—but they were doing well enough that they really trusted me and were listening to my ideas. Then two of the most significant things started to happen that made my career take off:

1. *Client Referrals.* There is no more positive thing that can happen to a financial advisor than to have a referral. It means that someone is happy with your work and wants to introduce you to friends and family. One of my best all time referrals came from Marvin, mentioned back in Chapter 2, who wanted to know about tax-free notes. He referred his friend Sandy, who was working with him as a business associate. Sandy, in turn, was one of my greatest sources of referrals over the years. This helped me grow my business and my credibility. Another great referral came from a competitor who knew me and referred to me a man named Hank, who was a CEO of NYSE-listed company. Hank became a great friend and he sent me Doug and Joan, and the list went on...

2. *Client Reassignments.* Because many aspiring brokers were leaving the business, the clients they had on the books were reassigned to the remaining brokers. Some of these people were wonderful, while others were disenchanted that their broker left were are not interested in working with you. I must have been blessed with people who many times found my approach refreshing, and I must say that a large segment of my long-term relationships came from these reassignments.

The more successful you become at a place like Merrill Lynch, the more perks and power start to come your way. When I started, five or six brokers would share a secretarial assistant, but when your production reached higher levels, you were rewarded with having your own staff people. One of the hardest working people in my world is Marcy Cahill, who worked with me for 32 out of the 34 years of my employment at Merrill. She is such a good person that clients would tell me that they could take or leave me, but they reminded me to never let Marcy get away. Luckily for the firm, she is younger than me and stayed on even after I left, but it was my good fortune to find such a great asset early in my career.

Not far behind Marcy was my longtime partner, Tom Melter, who had great gifts that are wonderfully suited to the investment world. We worked together, well, as I enjoyed doing things he wasn't thrilled about, and he did many things that I preferred not to do. Good partnerships involve many dynamics, but the most important dynamic is the simple math: $1 + 1 = 3$ or more! If you're joining together results only in the same productivity as the two of you individually, then the partnership may be a mistake. During my last two years at Merrill Lynch, the same math worked by adding Nancy Cox to the team, and clients are all the better for her presence.

I also had the assistance of two great people, Cathy Calvey and Steve Lull, along with many support staff from the downtown and Westside Cleveland Merrill Lynch offices. You can never be successful in a people business without having good support people to make you look good. I was the beneficiary of such qualified and dedicated people.

One of the great thrills for me was the day our son Blair called and asked if he could return to Cleveland and learn the business from me and join our team. He was calling from Jacksonville, Florida on one of the coldest days of an Ohio winter. He and his young wife, Joy, were living a few blocks from the ocean and were doing very well, both working at significant positions at the Merrill Lynch Mortgage Corporation.

"Why would you leave a great situation that you have built for two years there to start over as a financial advisor?" I asked him.

"I want to learn the business, and I want to learn it from you," he said. Fortunately for Blair, his wife agreed with the importance of that calling and despite her Texas roots, encouraged the move to Ohio. Now, he is my advisor, and I learn from him every time we talk! Although he and his family now live in San Antonio, he still commutes to Ohio each month to visit with clients. For the first seven years of his work on the advisory side of the business, we had the chance to learn and grow together, and, more importantly, he grew professionally with the team and people around him. I wish every father had the chance to see their children grow and advance as I did with Blair. He is living up to my prediction that he will be better at the task of being a financial advisor than his father. It was so significant for me to finish my career as he was starting his. They now have three boys, who keep them very busy; they are now a full-time job. Grandpa and Grandma go to Texas whenever possible to keep track of all of them.

We also have been blessed to have a daughter who is a special part of our family. An outstanding person in every way and an academic all-star, she was first in her high school class, graduated with honors from Duke and Georgetown Law School and holds a Ph.D. from Berkeley. She is now a law school professor at Georgetown Law School. She is married to an equally impressive husband, and they also have a son. We track them down in either Washington, D.C. or at their home in California to be a part of their lives. If you are involved in a lively discussion, it is almost always an advantage to have my daughter on your side!

My wife Marlene has been, without a doubt my biggest cheerleader. When I was contemplating a change from being a teacher and coach to being a financial advisor, it seemed like such a major shift in my gifts and my work. As I laid out the concerns about the difference in time schedules and demands that this new position would require, she was quite pragmatic about it:

"First," she said, "let's look at the time you are so concerned about. How much time are you looking at with the new job?"

"Long days, some nights and Saturdays during the first four or five years," I explained.

"What do you think your days and nights look like as a teacher and coach?"

"All day in the classroom, and every night with practices and games—but I get the summers off."

She reminded me that in four years I had not taken one summer "off" as I had actually taken full summer schedules to finish my master's degree.

"If this is what God wants you to do with your life, time will be provided for your family and the ministry activities of your life," she said

She was right, and her support in helping me in the home with the kids and in organizing our lives outside of work made all the difference for me to focus on God's calling. What a difference it makes when spouses can get on the same page and know that including God's will in all we do is a greater key to success than knowing how to sell an investment or any product.

One of my closest brothers in the Lord is the patriarch of Cuyahoga Valley Church in Broadview Heights, Ohio. Rick Duncan started the church there despite his family members lobbying him to take a church in Florida instead of Ohio. But he felt the Lord's calling, and he has influenced so many people through his teaching ministry. He also took some mornings to mentor me in the possibilities of adopting a move from success to significance as we read and shared together from the book *Half Time*, by Bob Buford. I am forever indebted to Rick for his example of sacrifice and service that encouraged me both professionally and in the area of missions.

Despite all the success and accolades from my career at Merrill Lynch, I am, at heart, still a small town kid from Delta, Ohio. It was unfortunate that my father died when I was just 15 years old and much of the farm work fell on my mother and me. My family (two older brothers and an older sister), teachers, and coaches from that era will always be special to me because they convinced me I could accomplish things if I worked hard and listened to credible instruction. My pastor while I was growing up, Gordon Zimmerman, was truly my hero. When he taught me that there is a difference between knowing about faith in Christ with my heart as opposed to faith with just my head, I wanted the heart's version. As I listened to so many great leaders in my life, there was a single passage that became my life's verse, Matthew 6:33: "*But seek first his kingdom and his righteousness, and all these things will be given to you as well.*"

How about you? Do you relate? Are you ready to take a hard look at your portfolio, call your financial advisor—and get a new one if need be—and start the screening process for your holdings? Let's get on the same page and start a movement in Biblically Responsible Investing.

If God owns it all—and He does—does your portfolio reflect that? In Matthew 16:26 Jesus reminded His disciples: "What good will it be for a man if he gains the whole world, yet forfeits his soul?"

The bottom line is easy to read and is undeniable: When we invest our money according to biblical principles, everyone profits. They are *Kingdom Gains.*

QUESTIONS TO CONSIDER

1. Do you identify with this author when he shares about his personal life?

2. How does your family influence the way you approach financial decisions?

3. When it comes to touching you at your point of need, what do you think this author failed to address? What struck a nerve?

4. If you were recommending this book to someone else, what would you say to describe why you think they would benefit from reading it?

APPENDICES

Appendix A

BRI Resources and Contact Information for Investors

National Association Christian Financial Consultants (NACFC)
www.nacfc.org
1055 Maitland Center Commons; Suite 100-B
Maitland, Florida 32751
(877) 966-2232

Kingdom Advisors
www.kingdomadvisors.org
(formerly Christian Financial Professionals Network (CFPN)
 www.cfpn.org)
5605 Glenridge Drive; Suite 845
Atlanta, Georgia 30342
(404) 497-7680

Generous Giving, Inc.
www.generousgiving.org
820 Broad Street; Suite 300
Chattanooga, Tennessee 37402
(423) 755-1640 (fax)

Christian Financial Association of America
Pat Hail, Pastor/Director of Development
Email: pathailjr@gmail.com
(830) 609-6986

Precept Ministries International
www.precept.org
7324 Noah Reid Road
Chattanooga, Tenn. 37422
(800) 763-8280

Crown Financial Ministries
www.crown.org
P.O. Box 100
Gainesville, Georgia 30503-0100
(800) 722-1976

Financial Peace University/ The Lampo Group
www.daveramsey.com
1749 Mallory Lane; Suite 100
Brentwood, Tennessee 37027
(888) 227-3223

In His Steps Foundation
Attn: Rob Cathcart
PO Box 23455
Chagrin Falls, Ohio 44023
(330) 528-1785

The National Christian Foundation
www.nationalchristian.com
11625 Rainwater Drive, Suite 500
Alpharetta, Georgia 30009
(800) 681-6223/(404) 252-0100 ph (404) 252-5177 fax

Interfaith Council for Corporate Responsibility (ICCR)
www.iccr.org
474 Riverside Drive Suite; Suite 1842
New York, NY 10115-0050
(212) 870-2294

APPENDIX B

BIBLICALLY-RESPONSIBLE INVESTING: THREE PERSONAL JOURNEYS

JOURNEY #1

By Daniel L Hardt, CLU, ChFC, CFP®, AAMS
Dan Hardt Financial Services
Louisville, KY

I can still remember right where I was standing, down the hall from my office when I heard a page and picked up a phone. It was the mid '90s, and a man named Art Ally was calling about a new mutual fund called The Timothy Plan. This fund screened out stocks of companies involved in abortion, pornography, gambling and other objectionable activities. As I primarily invest using mutual funds, it sounded interesting, but it was a new idea to me, and I was too busy and too scared just trying to make a go of things to give it much attention. I threw the idea into the back of my mind with all the other good, but unused, ideas.

Over the next few years I heard more about this concept through the National Association of Christian Financial Consultants (NACFC). Over time (through repetition more than spiritual enlightenment), I became more comfortable with it. But there weren't many screened funds to choose from so it was impossible to implement all the wonderful portfolio-building ideas I had been learning.

I began occasionally using the screened funds for smaller accounts. For larger accounts it seemed more important to use all my new modern portfolio strategies to build efficient portfolios. Using screened investments was not convenient for anything other than the smallest accounts because there was so little from which to pick. Though there was something morally compelling about it, I kept it in the back of my mind. It was just another arrow in my quiver to use here and there.

I had all the normal excuses for avoiding the moral reality of the issue: "In a mutual fund, I don't really directly own any of the 'bad' companies," and, "No company is really all pure," and, "One person's investment dollars aren't enough to really make any difference," and even, "To be a good steward, it mattered more that I invested with state-of-the-art methodologies than that I avoid companies that supported anti-Christian issues."

But I was ignoring obedience to God's Word, which tells me to avoid associations with evil. I also was ignoring the supply-and-demand issue—we would never have more resources for Biblically Responsible Investing until there was a demand from reps like me. And I also was ignoring my leadership role with clients: They won't know what's going on inside their funds unless I tell them— *and they have a right to know.*

I had evolved to the point where, when working with Christian clients, I would describe screened investments. I would dispassionately describe the moral value of screening and also describe the "costs" to invest in this way. The client could decide if they wanted to "invest with moral values" or not.

One day I was meeting with a new client. She was Christian and a young widow. My brother, for whom she worked, referred her to me. She had some money to invest, and I objectively described biblically-screened investing and all its value and costs as well as the regular alternatives. I did such a wonderful job of being impartial that she wasn't sure which to choose. She said, "Whenever I'm working for your brother, and we're trying to decide what to do, your brother says, 'what's the right thing to do?' So, Dan, for my investments, what's the right thing to do?"

To this day I wonder if she noticed the watering in my eyes as I absorbed her question, "What's the right thing to do?" The answer was obvious. The answer was always obvious, but I had only been doing a moral tap-dance with the issue for all these years –using biblically-screened investments as a convenience, a warm fuzzy option to which some Christians would be drawn.

I have found that most Christian clients do care about this issue (when we make them aware of it) and want to invest in ways that are in line with biblical priorities. I'm doing a better job of making sure I provide leadership regarding this issue for my clients. A big step in the right direction for me was to make sure my own investments were invested in biblically-sound funds.

I still have a long way to go regarding this issue. It's been harder than I want to admit to adjust the methods I use to build investment portfolios to fit the limitations that morally-screened investing demands. And what about all those clients from prior years whose investments still support abortion, pornography, gambling and other issues that make my heart ache (and God's heart also)?

I know some financial advisors who will not knowingly invest any money for any client (whether Christian or not) that involves companies that support any of these objectionable issues. I'm not at that point yet, thinking that, especially for non-Christian clients, it's more important to acquire the client first and possibly "convert" them later. But I admit I am not at peace with this position. I'm not sure I want to look Jesus in the face and try to explain my rationale.

I'm counting on you. We must support each other as we travel this counter-cultural path. I'm prayerful that, through groups like Kingdom Advisors and NACFC, we can continue to grow in our willingness to follow Christ regarding this issue as we use our practices for His glory.

JOURNEY #2

By Clifford Gill
Associate Regional Director
PennMutual Insurance Company

As a former wholesaler for OneAmerica and now currently the associate regional director for PennMutual Insurance Company, my responsibility is to meet and generate interest (business) in our products. When I first started working at OneAmerica, I called on any financial advisor or insurance agent who would see me. However, many advisors only agreed to meet with me if I bought them lunch or gave them a small sum of money to support their client events or marketing promotions. There were even requests from some advisors to meet after hours at bars, strip clubs and gambling casinos. I felt uncomfortable in those establishments and rejected all such offers, thus ending my relationship with a number of advisors. I adjusted my activities to meet with those genuinely interested in working ethically and who advertised themselves as following biblical principles. However, I soon learned that many of these advisors claimed to be Christians but were more interested in earning commissions than in helping their clients or promoting biblical principles. Bending and often breaking NASD rules and God's Commandments were common sales practices. I felt frustrated and considered leaving this business to pursue a more ethical line of work. During this period, I prayed frequently for divine guidance.

Then in 2004 I met Glenn Repple, who heads a Christian broker-dealer, G.A. Repple, outside of Orlando, Florida. Glenn attracts highly ethical advisors, the majority of whom place God and their clients ahead of themselves. Glenn personally introduced me to his advisors in my territory. Working with a group of professionals who do our business the right way inspired and motivated me to stay in the business and seek out other ethical advisors outside of G.A. Repple. I asked Glenn for help, and he introduced me to Art Ally, president of The Timothy Funds. The Timothy Funds office is located just a few minutes from Glenn's office. The Timothy Funds are a family of mutual funds that promote biblically- based investing by excluding companies supporting abortion, pornography, same-sex lifestyles, gambling, tobacco and alcohol. Art and his staff introduced me to several Christian advisors who promote investing based on biblical principles. At each meeting with these advisors, I felt increasingly committed to stay in the business and promote biblical principles. After consulting with Glenn and Art, I strongly believed that OneAmerica should include some of the Timothy Funds inside their variable products. Getting a corporate bureaucracy to change is not easy, but in May of 2005, two of the Timothy Funds were added to OneAmerica's sub-accounts. Currently, only OneAmerica offers the Timothy Funds inside their variable products.

God, through Art Ally and Glenn Repple, then led me to Ron Blue in Atlanta, Georgia. Ron heads Kingdom Advisors, a networking organization of more than a thousand Christian financial advisors. Interestingly, many of the advisors I called on were under G.A. Repple's broker-dealer, sold The Timothy Funds and belonged to Kingdom Advisors. I was able to enhance many relationships and received numerous referrals of other Christian advisors. More importantly, OneAmerica became a corporate founding partner of Kingdom Advisors. One of the benefits of this relationship is participation at Kingdom Advisors's annual conference, which allowed me to meet additional Christian advisors.

When I was at the low point in my career, I prayed and God answered. Now, I call on ethical advisors regardless of faith. I receive more referrals than I can handle and am blessed with an income that far exceeds my needs. Matthew 7:7 says, "Ask and you will receive." In my case, what I received was more than I could ever believe.

JOURNEY #3

By Russell Winstead
Solomon Financial Group

I began my financial services career at Merrill Lynch; my previous background among other things was being a pastor and minister. To me "Biblically Responsible Investing" (BRI) seemed to be a "no brainer" for believers, for advisors and the Wall Street firms and others that offer investments. I had owned Timothy Funds myself for a few years before going into the business, and although at that time the performance was not as good as it is today, my feelings were that even though I may earn a little less return than some of the non-screened funds, the Lord would bless in a greater way the returns I did receive.

But, to my surprise, at that time, no one seemed to get it! Not the investors, not the advisors and not the firms. It then occurred to me that this was not about what made sense or what was an appropriate investment, it was spiritual warfare! The enemy knew the advancement the kingdom could make as investments are diverted away from the companies that promote ungodly ways to companies that support a pro-biblical/community approach as well as the mindset of faith, in putting God first in our investments.

My partner and I worked with other folks inside Merrill Lynch, like Dwight Short in an effort to offer what we knew would be a great product offering for both our clients and the company.

However, although progress was made, our pushing and constant encouragement to include these funds along with other biblical values issues led to an environment that was not conducive to a continued relationship with ML. In other words, they were sick of hearing about it, and our time at ML was running out. To sum it up, we were called to offer a godly practice, and at the time we could not do what we felt was right to do at ML so we needed to move on.

We then connected with Glenn at G.A. Repple & Company and started Solomon Financial Group. We help clients make wise decisions about their money, including BRI, using Timothy Funds and other biblical-decision approaches.

AND to the glory of God, and to the credit of many previous and current Merrill Lynch advisors, ML does now offer Timothy Funds! Some may think that along the lines of logic, this would be a disappointment to me and others, since many of us had to leave ML to offer BRI, and now they finally offer it in competitive situation to us as independents. However, I view it as a great victory for the Kingdom and for all of us who have worked and prayed for Biblically Responsible Investing to become a mainstream offering.

And, as stated above, it's not just about investing; it is about the difference in spiritual mindset that Biblically Responsible Investing provides.

APPENDIX C

COMPANIES OFFERING BRI SERVICES

An updated copy of this listing can be found at http://www. KingdomGains.com/BRIServices.html Name changes and objectives of firms may change so check carefully before making investment decisions.

MF= mutual fund
SA= separate account mgr
TKI= turn key investments
ETF = exchange traded funds
MBI = mission based investments
ST =screening tools)

The Timothy Plan Mutual Funds (MF)
1055 Maitland Center Commons
Maitland, Florida 32751
(800) 846-7526
www.timothyplan.com

Stewardship Partners   (SA)
P. O. Box 157
Matthews, North Carolina 28106-0157
(800) 930-6949
www.stewardshippartners.com

Biblically Responsible Investing Institute (BRII) (ST)
P. O. Box 157
Matthews, North Carolina 28106-0157
(800) 930-6949
www.briinstitute.com

American Values Investments, Inc. (SA)
1321 Sunset Drive, Suite 23
Johnson City, Tennessee 37604
(423) 722-1776
www.americanvalues.com

CAMCO Investors Fund (Cornerstone Management) (MF)
Cornerstone Asset Management, Inc.
30 E. Main Street
Berryville, Virginia 22611
(800) 727-1007
www.camcofunds.com   Info@CamcoFunds.com

Ave Maria Mutual Funds (MF)
3707 W. Maple Road; Suite 100
Bloomfield Hills, Michigan 48301
C/o Schwartz Investment Trust
(866) 283-6274
www.avemariafund.com   corourke@schwartzinvest.com

The Steward Mutual Funds (MF)
Capstone Asset Management & Planning Co.
5847 San Felipe Street
Houston, Texas 77057
(800) 262-6631
www.stewardmutualfunds.com
info@stewardfundconsulting.com

Eventide Gilead Fund (MF)
c/o Matrix Capital Group, Inc.
630-a Fitwatertown Road 2nd Floor
Willow Grove PA, 19090-1904
info@eventidefunds.coml

GuideStone Funds (MF) (restricted to Southern Baptist entities)
C/o PFPC
PO Box 9834
Providence, Rhode Island 02940-8034
(888) 984-8433
www.guidestonefunds.org

FaithShares Inc. (ETF)
3555 Northwest 58th Street, Suite 410
Oklahoma City, Oklahoma 73112
1-877-FAITH55
www.faithshares.com

Moral Money (ST)
www.moralmoney.com

Moral Money is a site dedicated to expanding the awareness of Biblically Responsible Investing and helping people grow closer to Christ by illuminating the biblical insights of investment stewardship. Biblically Responsible Investing is the act of building an investment portfolio consisting only of companies that do not participate in or promote lifestyles that are offensive to Christian values.

The information provided in this Appendix and throughout the book Kingdom Gains is for the benefit of the reader, and no approval or endorsement is intended by listing on these pages. Listings are for information only and not a solicitation to buy or sell any securities. Readers should obtain a prospectus and consult their advisors

APPENDIX D

COMPARING BRI FINANCIAL PERFORMANCE

Performance is often the most abused statistical tactic in the investment world to justify one's position. The objective of *Kingdom Gains* is to help investors to find and interpret investment performance. Consequently, the best information is the most current information. By visiting each BRI provider listed in Appendix B, investors should be able to find up-to-date statistics along with their benchmarks. The rules for interpreting performance are the same whether looking at BRI providers or any investment. Here are some guidelines for interpretation:

1. Look at performance over short, intermediate and long time periods.
2. Try to compare with other investments that have similar objectives.
3. When possible, make sure to use the same metric, such as "time weighted rate of return" or "dollar weighted rate of return."
4. Determine if the benchmark(s) being used are compatible with the investments being measured.
5. Determine what your needs are to know how often to be concerned about performance—no less than yearly and no more than monthly.
6. Establish an action plan based on what will happen if performance is better or poorer than expected.

7. Make certain when comparing investment choices to use performance data over the same time periods and calculated in the same manner.

RESOURCES

Nabor, Mary (now under married name of King, Mary). "Christ's Returns." *Christianity Today*, September 3, 2001.

Hightlights from her article: "...*Restored in freedom of God's grace, we can seek to give our accounting: 'Master, your money was multiplied many times over. In addition, I was a witness to your light in the world by providing beneficial products for my neighbor. I voted company proxies according to my conscience. And I helped build a church...Your kingdom was extended in 10 ways at once!'*"

"... *Academic research demonstrates that screening, or the exclusion of certain industries from stock portfolios, does not significantly affect financial returns.*"

Camejo, Peter. *The SRI Advantage.* Gabriola Island, B.C.: New Society Publishers, 2002.

Guerard, John B. "Is There a Cost to Being Socially Responsible In Investing?" *Journal of Investing.* Summer, 1997.

Domini 400 Social Index. Inception in May 1990 and has shown performance advantages in most periods against the S&P 500 and Russell 1000 Indexes.

Domini, Amy. *Socially Responsible Investing.* Chicago: Dearborn Trade, 2001

Sparkes, Russell. *Socially Responsible Investing: A Global Revolution.* Sussex: John Wiley & Sons, Ltd. 2002.

Appendix E

Contact Information for the S&P 100

This information is included at the suggestion of my good friend, Gordon Heffern, who will have to read this book from heaven. He was my friend and colleague in ministry in many organizations and read excerpts from my book and offered many thoughts and encouragements.

The S&P 100 Index is copyright Standard & Poor's Financial Services LLC, www.indices.standardandpoors.com and is used with permission.

Abbott Labs
100 Abbot Park Road
Abbott Park, IL 60064-3500
(847)937-6100 ph (847)937-1511 fax
www.abbott.com

Alcoa
201 Isabella Street
Pittsburg, PA 15212-5858
(412)553-4545 ph (412)553-4498 fax
www.alcoa.com

Allstate Corporation
2775 Sanders Road
Northbrook, IL 60062-6127
(847)402-5000 ph (847)402-2351 fax
www.allstate.com

Altria Group
120 Park Avenue 15th Floor
New York, NY 10017
(917)663-4000 ph (917)878-2167 fax
www.altria.com

Amazon Com
1516 2nd Avenue
Seattle, WA 98101-1543
(206)622-2335
www.amazon.com

American Electric Power
1 Riverside Plaza
Columbus, OH 43215-2372
(614)716-1000 ph (614)223-1823 fax
www.aep.com

American Express
World Financial Center
200 Vesey Street
New York, NY 10285
(212)640-2000 ph (212)619-9230 fax
www.americanexpress.com

Amgen
One Amgen Center Drive
Thousand Oaks, CA 91320-1799
(805)447-1000 ph (805)447-1010 fax
Investor.relations@amgen.com

Apple Inc.
1 Infinite Loop
MS 301 41R
Cupertino, CA 95014
(408)996-1010 ph (408)996-0275 fax
www.apple.com

AT&T
175 East Houston Street
San Antonio, TX 78205-2255
(210)821-4105 ph (314)331-9896 fax
www.att.com

Avon Products
1345 Avenue of the Americas
New York, NY 10105-0196
(212)282-5000 ph (212)282-6035 fax
www.avon.com

Baker Hughes Inc.
Suite 2100
2929 Allen Parkway
Houston, TX 77019-2118
(713)349-8600 ph (713)359-8699 fax
www.bakerhughesdirect.com

Bank of America
100 North Tryon Street
Charlotte, NC 28255
(704)386-5681 ph (704)386-6699 fax
www.bankofamerica.com

BNY Mellon
One Wall Street
New York, NY 10286
(212)495-1784
www.bnymellon.com

Baxter International
One Baxter Parkway
Deerfield, IL 60015-4633
(847)948-2000 ph (847)948-3948 fax
www.baxter.com

Berkshire Hathaway Inc.
Suite 1440
3555 Farnam Street
Omaha, NE 68131
(402)346-1400 ph
www.berkshirehathaway.com

Boeing Company
100 North Riverside
Chicago, IL 60606
(312)544-2000 ph (312)544-2082 fax
www.boeing.com

Bristol Myers Squibb
345 Park Avenue
New York, NY 10154
(212)546-4000 ph (212)546-4020 fax
www.bms.com

CVS/Caremark
One CVS Drive
Woonsocket, RI 02895
(401))765-1500 ph (401)765-2137 fax
www.cvs.com

Campbell Soup
One Campbell Place
Camden, NJ 08103 1799
(856)342-4800 ph (856)342-3878 fax
www.campbellsoupcompany.com

Capital One Financial
1680 Capital One Drive
McLean, VA 22102
(703)720-1000 ph (703)205-1755 fax
www.capitalone.com

Caterpillar Inc.
100 NE Adams Street
Peoria, IL 61629
(309)675-6155 ph (309)675-6155 fax
www.cat.com

Chevron Corporation
6001 Bollinger Canyon Road
San Ramon, CA 94583
(925)842-1000 ph (415)894-6817 fax
www.chevron.com

Cisco Systems
170 West Tasman Drive
San Jose, CA 95134
(408)526-4000 ph (408)526-4100 fax
www.cisco.com

Citigroup
399 Park Avenue
New York, NY 10043
(212)559-1000 ph (212)793-3946 fax
www.citigroup.com

Coca Cola
One Coca-Cola Plaza
Atlanta, GA 30313
(404)676-2121 ph (404)676-6792 fax
www.cocacola.com

Colgate Palmolive
300 Park Avenue
New York, NY 10022
(212)310-2000 ph (212)310-3284 fax
www.colgate.com

Comcast Corporation
1500 Market Street
philadel phia, PA 19102-2148
(215)667-1700 ph (215)981-1790 fax
www.comcast.com

Conoco Phillips
600 North Dairy Ashford
Houston, TX 77079
(281)293-1000 ph (281)293-1440 fax
www.conoco phillips.com

Costco
P.O. Box 343311
Issaquah, WA 98027
(206)313-6416 ph
www.costco.com

Dell Inc.
One Dell Way
Round Rock, TX 78682
(512)338-4400 ph (512)728-3653 fax
www.dell.com

Devon Energy Corporation
20 N. Broadway
Oklahoma City, OK 73102
(405)552-4526 ph
www.devonenergy.com

Disney
500 S. Buena Vista Street
Burbank, CA 91521
(818)560-1000 ph (818)560-1930 fax
www.disney.com

Dow Chemical
2030 Dow Center
Midland, MI 48674
(989)636-1000 ph (989)636-4033 fax
www.dow.com

DuPont
1007 Market Street
Wilmington, DE 19898
(302)774-1000 ph (302)773-2631 fax
www.dupont.com

EMC Corporation
176 South Street
Hopkinton, MA 01748
(508)435-1000 ph (508)435-5222 fax
www.emc.com

Entergy
639 Loyola Avenue
New Orleans, LA 70113
(504)576-4000 ph (507)576-4428 fax
www.entergy.com

Exelon Corporation
10 S. Dearborn St., 37th Floor
Box 805379
Chicago, IL 60680-5379
(312)394-7398 ph (312)394-7345 fax
www.exeloncorp.com

Exxon Mobil
5959 Las Colinas Blvd.
Irving, TX 75039-2298
(972)444-1000 ph (972)444-1348 fax
www.exxonmobil.com

FedEx Corp
942 S. Shady Grove Road
Mem phis, TN 38120
(901)818-7500 ph
www.fedex.com

Ford Motor
One American Road
Dearborn, MI 48126
(313)322-3000 ph (313)845-7512 fax
www.ford.com

Freeport McMoran
1 N. Central Avenue
phoenix, AZ 85004
(602)366-8100 ph

General Dynamics
2941 Fairview Park Drive, Suite 100
Falls Church, VA 22042-4153
(703)876-3000 ph (703)876-3125 fax
www.generaldynamics.com

General Electric
3135 Easton Turnpike
Fairfield, CT 06828-0001
(203)373-2211 ph (203)373-3131 fax
www.ge.com

Gilead Sciences
333 Lakeside Drive
Foster City, CA 94404
(650)574-3000 ph (650)522-5853 fax
www.gilead.com

Goldman Sachs
85 Broad Street
New York, NY 10004
(212)902-1000 ph (212)902-3000 fax
www.gs.com

Google Inc.
1600 Am phitheatre Parkway
Mountain View, CA 94043
(650)253-0000 ph (650)253-0001 fax
www.google.com

Halliburton
5 Houston Center
1401 McKinney Suite 2400
Houston, TX 77010
(713)759-2688 ph (713)759-2635 fax
www.halliburton.com

Heinz
600 Grant Street
Pittsburg, Pennsylvania 15219
(412)456-5700 ph (412)456-6015 fax
www.heinz.com

Hewlett Packard
3000 Hanover St.
Palo Alto, CA 94304
(650)857-1501 ph (650)857-5518 fax
www.hp.com

Home Depot
2455 Paces Ferry Road NW
Atlanta, Georgia 30339
(770)433-8211 ph (770)431-2685 fax
www.homedepot.com

Honeywell International
110 Columbia Road
Morris Township, NJ 07962
(973)455-2000 ph (973)455-2096 fax
www.honeywell.com

Intel Corp
2200 Mission College Boulevard
Santa Clara, CA 95052-8119
(408)765-8080 ph (408)765-9904 fax
www.intel.com

IBM
1 New Orchard Road
Armond, NJ 10504
(914)499-1900 ph (914)765-7382 fax
www.ibm.com

JP Morgan Chase
270 Park Avenue
New York, NY 10017
(212)270-6000 ph (212)270-1648 fax
www.jpmorgancase.com

Johnson & Johnson
One Johnson & Johnson Plaza
New Brunswick, NJ 08933
(732)524-0400 ph (732)214-0332 fax
www.jnj.com

Kraft Foods Inc.
Three Lakes Drive
Northfield, IL 60093
(847)646-2000 ph (847)646-6005 fax
www.kraft.com

Lockheed Martin
(301)897-6455 ph
www.lockheedmartin.com

Lowe's Corp
1000 Lowe's Boulevard
Mooresville, North Carolina 28115
(704)758-1000 ph
www.lowes.com

Mastercard, Inc.
2200 MasterCard Blvd.
O'Fallon, Missouri 63368-7263
(636)722-6100 ph
www.mastercard.com

McDonalds Corp.
2111 McDonalds Drive
Oak Brook, IL 60523
(630)623-3000 ph (630)623-5211 fax
www.mcdonalds.com

Medtronic Inc
710 Medtronic Parkway
Minneapolis, MN 55432
(763)514-4000 ph (763)514-4879 fax
www.medtronic.com

Merck & Co.
Box 1000 One Merck Drive
Whitehouse St, NJ 08889-0100
(908)423-1000 ph (908)735-1253 fax
www.merck.com

MetLife, Inc.
200 Park Ave.
New York, NY 10166
(212)578-2211 ph (212)578-3320 fax
www.metlife.com

Microsoft
One Microsoft Way
Redmond, WA 98052-6399
(425)882-8080 ph (425)936-7329 fax
www.microsoft.com

Monsanto Company
800 N. Lindbergh Boulevard
St. Louis, Missouri 63167
(314)694-1000 ph (314)694-8394 fax
www.monsanto.com

Morgan Stanley
1585 Broadway
New York, NY 10036
(212)761-4000 ph (212)761-0086 fax
www.morganstanley.com

National Oilwell Varco, Inc.
7909 Parkwood Circle Dr.
Houston, TX 77036
(713)375-3700 ph
www.nov.com

News Corporation
1211 Avenue of the Americas
New York, NY 10036
(212)852-7017 ph

NIKE Corporation
One Bowerman Drive
Beaverton, Oregon 97005
(800)344-6453 ph (503)671-6453 ph
www.nike.com

Norfolk Southern
Three Commercial Place
Norfolk, VA 23510-2191
(757)629-2680 ph (757)629-2361 fax
www.nscorp.com

NYSE Euronext
11 Wall Street
New York, NY 10005-1905
(212)656-3000 ph
www.nyse.com

Occidental Petroleum
1230 Avenue of the Americas
New York, NY 10020
(212)603-8111 ph
www.oxy.com

Oracle Corporation
500 Oracle Parkway
Redmond City, CA 94065
(650)506-7000 ph (650)506-7200 fax
www.oracle.com

PepsiCo Inc.
700 Anderson Hill Road
Purchase, NY 10577
(914)253-2000 ph (914)253-2070fax
www.pepsico.com

Pfizer Inc.
235 E. 42nd Street
New York, NY 10017
(212)573-2323 ph (212)573-7851 fax
www.pfizer.com

Philip Morris International
120 Park Avenue
New York, NY 10017
(917)663 2233 ph
www.pmi.com

Procter & Gamble
One Procter and Gamble Plaza
Cincinnati, OH 45202
(513)983-1100 ph (513)983-4381 fax
www.pg.com

Qualcomm Inc.
5775 Morehouse Drive
San Diego, CA 92121
(858)587-1121 ph
www.qualcomm.com

Raytheon Company
870 Winter Street
Waltham, MA 02451
(781)522-3000 ph (781)860-2172 fax
www.raytheon.com

Regions Financial
1900 Fifth Avenue North
Birmingham, AL 35203
(205)994-1300 ph (901)58-3915 fax
www.regions.com

Sara Lee
3500 Lacey Road
Downers Grove, IL 60515
(630)598-6000 ph (635)598-8482 fax
www.saralee.com

Schlumberger
5599 San Felipe 27th Floor
Houston, TX 77056
(713)513-2000 ph (713)513-2006 fax
www.slb.com

Southern Co
30 Ivan Allen Jr. Boulevard NW
Atlanta, Georgia 30308
(404)506-5000 ph
www.southernco.com

Sprint Nextel
2001 Edmund Halley Drive
Reston, VA 20191
(703)433-4000 ph (703)433-4343 fax
www.sprint.com

Target Corporation
100 Nicollet Mall
Minneapolis, MN 55403
(612)304-6073 ph (612)370-5502 fax
www.targetcorp.com

Texas Instruments
12500 Ti Boulevard
Box 660199
Dallas, TX 75266-0199
(972)995-3773 ph (972)995-4360 fax
www.ti.com

3M Company
3-M Center
St. Paul, MN 55144
(651)733-1110 ph (651)737-3061 fax
www.3m.com

Time Warner
One Time Warner Center
New York, NY 10019
(212)484-8000 ph (212)489-6183 fax
www.timewarner.com

United Healthcare Services Inc.
5901 Lincoln Dr
Minneapolis, MN 55436
(952)992-7777 ph
www.uhc.com

United Parcel Service Inc.
55 Glenlake Parkway NE
Atlanta, Georgia 30328
(404)828-6000 ph (404)828-7666 fax
www.ups.com

United Technologies
One Financial Plaza
Hartford, CT 06101
(860)728-7000 ph (860)728-7028 fax
www.utc.com

US Bancorp
800 Nicollet Mall
Minneapolis, MN
(612)303-0783 ph (612)303-0782 fax
www.usbank.com

Verizon Communications
140 West Street
New York, NY 10007
(212)395-1000 ph
www.verizon.com

Walgreens
200 Wilmot Road
Deerfield, IL 60015
(847)914-2500 ph
www.walgreens.com

Wal-Mart
702 SW Eighth Street
Bentonville, AR 72716
(479)273-4000 ph (479)273-4053 fax
www.walmartstores.com

Wells Fargo
420 Montgomery Street
San Francisco, CA 94104
(866)249-3302 ph (651)450-4033 fax
www.wellsfargo.com

Weyerhaeuser Co
33663 Weyerhaeuser Way South
Federal Way, WA 98003
(253)924-2345 ph 253)924-3543 fax
www.weyerhaeuser.com

Williams Cos
One Williams Center
Tulsa, OK 74172
(918)573-2000 ph (918)573-6714 fax
www.williams.com

Xerox Corporation
800 Long Ridge Road
Box 1600
Stamford, CT 06904-1600
(203)968-3000 ph (203)968-3218 fax
www.xerox.com

Websites often will change and using other web search engines may be helpful in finding the information you are seeking.

Check company human resources websites to access information you need.

APPENDIX F

SAMPLE LETTERS

Sample Letters can be downloaded from:
http://www.KingdomGains.com/sampleletters.html

[This letter is intended for sending to a company of which you are a current shareholder]

[your personal letter head]

[Date]

Dear Sir or Madam:

As a shareholder in [name of company] I am very grateful for all the efforts that management makes to achieve great results for all of us. As a Christian, I believe the responsibility for me to know that the activities of companies I hold in my portfolio, must be held to a higher standard. I know that there are no perfect companies any more than there are perfect people, but I would like to know if (name of company) is engaged in any of the following activities:

1. [List all of the issues that are relative to **YOUR** faith journey... abortion services, alcohol, tobacco, gaming, pornographic entertainment, military and munitions or others you may wish to include.]
2. Does our company encourage traditional family values?

3. Please clarify for me how much you estimate the current stock option plans for [name of company] have cost shareholders over the past three years and how this cost compares to our net earnings for the same period.
4. Can you clarify if [name of company] is a donor to Planned Parenthood or to Gay/Lesbian/Transgender organizations? If the answer is yes, can you indicate the approximate amount of such donations?

I appreciate very much the fact that we live in a pluralistic society with many different lifestyles and approaches to morality. I respect all of the different points of view in that regard because my Savior also loves every person, as we all are created in God's image and His love extends to everyone. But I am a short-term steward of the wealth that God has blessed me with, and I would want to know that in holding [name of company] stock, I am not violating my relationship with God. Your help in clarifying [name of company]'s positions on all of these issues would be most helpful. Thank You!

Sincerely,
[Your name here]

[Send to custodian, trustees or management teams for your retirement or other trusteed accounts]

[your personal letter head]

[Date]

Dear Sir or Madam:

Thank you for all your efforts to provide investment alternatives for me in planning for my [retirement/savings/other uses you might have]. As I consider the choices you have structured for me in the current plan, I have not been able to identify any funds or choices that are in line with my moral and spiritual convictions. Many of the funds hold stocks in companies that provide or encourage abortions, sell tobacco, alcohol and gaming services. Other holdings have positions in companies that profit from pornography and encourage non-traditional family lifestyles.

As a Christian, it is imperative that I try my best to reflect the same values in my investing as I attempt to do in my own life, and the lack of investment alternatives with a biblical perspective leaves me with a large void in choosing funds and investments.

Will you please let me know if I have missed investments that are currently available that you believe would accomplish this objective? If there are no such funds available, I would please request that you consider asking your financial people to recommend alternatives that would allow someone like me to know that is a future choice?

Sincerely,

[Your name here]
[Your title here]

Acknowledgements

National Association of Christian Financial Consultants (NACFC) was the first group to challenge me in my walk of faith to make my financial practice my ministry.

Kingdom Advisors

This group helped me grow in the process of learning how best to incorporate my faith into my work as a financial advisor. It has resources that appeal to both the large and the small firms.

Evangelical Mennonite Church

This is the church I grew up in and who taught me what it meant to become a disciple of Christ. The guidance that I received there in biblical instruction from teachers and parishioners has influenced me for a lifetime.

Middleburg Heights United Church of Christ

I gained significant growth as a young adult and father by being part of this church, despite its presence in a very liberal denomination. There are great Christian men and women in all of our mainstream churches who must stand tall in the midst of all the turmoil and challenges to traditional faith and family values

Cuyahoga Valley Church

If growth is a measure of one's faith, being part of CVC has helped me grow to twice my former height. Coming in as a believer for many years, CVC still taught me the importance of unconditional love and the importance of sharing the gospel around the world. The people and staff of CVC never stop finding ways to be part of the community and to share their faith by actions, words and music. I was hungry spiritually, and they fed me and helped me mature in my faith.

IDLEWILD BAPTIST CHURCH

This is my current church home in Lutz, Florida and the outreach in our community is a new breath of fresh air to all who participate in the life of our church. The passion to see people come to Christ is unparalleled, and the ability to bring people who have left the church back into faith is so great!

IN HIS STEPS FOUNDATION

Seeing how we can help others to learn about and implement stewardship in their lives and for the benefit of many ministries has been a thrill for me. A major goal of *Kingdom Gains* is to see more people become deliberate in their giving and estate planning to include God's work in their plans.

FELLOWSHIP OF CHRISTIAN ATHLETES

No organization has been as influential for me, for so long as FCA. Seeing the impact athletes have made over the years, also brings out the desire of my heart to see financial advisors have the same courage and conviction, going forward.

WOLGEMUTH & ASSOCIATES

Robert and Andrew Wolgemuth encouraged me as a young and inexperienced writer to have faith that the process works and the people who can benefit from reading my work will eventually do so.

MY FAMILY

Listening to my countless exchanges about the "book" and all the research required to present a message like *Kingdom Gains* requires a lot of patience. Thanks for all of your tolerance in dealing with my delusions of being an author!

MERRILL LYNCH

Despite all of the negative images that Wall Street projects, I am deeply impressed and indebted to all of the people who made my career a success. Even now, there are so many believers who also are financial advisors who are trying to make their practice more like their ministry, and each of their witnesses inspires me. In addition, there were so many people who supported me in my work there and made me look good. From my sales support team of Marcy, Steve and Cathy, to all of the operations team, I will always be indebted for their support of my work.

COMPUTER SUPPORT

My partner Tom Melter has been incredibly patient with my technical skills, both while I was working with him at Merrill Lynch, and even after my retirement. My neighbor, Bill Vitez has always been ready to help with any project I have given him, and he has always handled each task with great care and meticulous attention to detail. When all else fails, my son Blair always bails me out of problems that go beyond everyone else. Thanks to all of the above!

KIMA JUDE

Kima has helped me with editing, re-writes upon re-writes, and countless details in both the manuscript stage and the final edition.

ACKNOWLEDGEMENTS

GREGG SHORT

My nephew and newly crowned publisher has been a great young partner in helping me to get the message of BRI into the hands of thousands of people. Thanks also to his wife Gwen for working on the layout and final details of the publication. Thanks to ALL!

MONDAY MORNING MESSAGE READERS!

Many who are reading this book have been faithful and loyal weekly readers and bloggers of my MMMs, and the encouragement and input have been priceless!

FRIENDS & ASSOCIATES WHO HAVE PROOFREAD MY WORK

So many of you have offered your time and insights to improve my words and thoughts. Specifically I'd like to thank Kinney Cathart for proofreading the entire book. If you were able to help proofread, this book is part of your testimony as well! Thanks!

ABOUT THE AUTHOR

Dwight L. Short, Retired (1971-2005), First Vice President-Investments, Merrill Lynch
- CIMA (Certified Investment Management Analyst) CIMA
- CFM (Certified Financial Manager, ML)
- Wealth Management Advisor

Dwight grew up on a family farm in Delta, Ohio and has three siblings. His mother was a schoolteacher, and his father farmed. He graduated from Bowling Green State University (1967) as a math major and Case Western Reserve (1970) where he obtained his MBA in banking and finance. At Merrill Lynch, his practice emphasis was a dual relationship with individual and institutional clients to convert complex strategies into easy to understand choices for sophisticated clients, and those not familiar with the capital markets.

In 1999, Dwight became a member of the National Association of Christian Financial Consultants and a member of Kingdom Advisors in 2005. He is a founding trustee of In His Steps Foundation, a Christian Community Foundation. He continues to help in a variety of ministry activities in Northeast Ohio. He has been an active member of Cuyahoga Valley Community Church, CVCC (Broadview Hts., Ohio) since the mid 1990s, and has participated on several different mission trips. He is currently attending Idlewild Baptist Church in Lutz (Tampa), Florida, while supporting the Kingdom Advisors activities in the Tampa area.

Dwight has published a weekly devotional known as the Monday Morning Message (MMM) on his website DLSConsult.com since 2003. The MMM speaks to varied subjects including financial news: sports news: and most of all biblical truth from real life situations. This experience was instrumental in a sense of calling for Dwight to take on a significant project in writing *Kingdom Gains*.

Book Website Address
http://www.KingdomGains.com

- Purchase additional copies of this book on the website

- Errata (errors/revisions):
  http://www.KingdomGains.com/Errata

- Cataloging in Publication (CIP) Data
  http://www.KingdomGains.com/CIP

- Sample Letters
  http://www.KingdomGains.com/SampleLetters

- BRI Service Providers
  http://www.KingdomGains.com/BRIServices

- Special Online only content

- Sign-up for information on the forthcoming Study Guide

LaVergne, TN USA
26 November 2010

206193LV00004B/1/P